PLYMOUTH COUNTY MARRIAGES

1692-1746

LITERALLY TRANSCRIBED FROM THE FIRST VOLUME OF THE
RECORDS OF THE INFERIOR COURT OF COMMON PLEAS,
AND FROM AN UNNUMBERED VOLUME AND VOLUME
ONE OF THE RECORDS OF THE COURT OF
GENERAL SESSIONS OF THE PEACE,
PLYMOUTH COUNTY,
MASSACHUSETTS

REPRINTED FROM VOLUMES ONE AND TWO OF " THE GENEALOGICAL ADVERTISER "

1898-1899

CAMBRIDGE, MASS.
LUCY HALL GREENLAW, PUBLISHER
1900

Notice

In many older books, foxing (or discoloration) occurs and, in some instances, print lightens with wear and age. Reprinted books, such as this, often duplicate these flaws, notwithstanding efforts to reduce or eliminate them. The pages of this reprint have been digitally enhanced and, where possible, the flaws eliminated in order to provide clarity of content and a pleasant reading experience.

Originally published
Cambridge, Mass.
1900

Reprinted by:

Janaway Publishing, Inc.
732 Kelsey Ct.
Santa Maria, California 93454
(805) 925-1038

http://www.JanawayGenealogy.com

2012

ISBN: 9781596412750

Made in the United States of America

NOTE.

The publication of Plymouth County Marriages was begun in THE GENEALOGICAL ADVERTISER in March, 1898, and the sheets of this pamphlet were reprinted from that magazine from time to time as the several installments appeared. It was the intention of the publisher to issue an indexed volume of these marriages as soon as their publication in the magazine was completed. The fact that these records were being printed was generally known, and has been widely advertised during the past three years. Rev. Frederic W. Bailey, B. D., "Member New England *Genealogical* and *Biographical* Society," has recently forestalled the balance of this intended work by publishing abstracts of the larger part of the Plymouth County Marriages, as the second volume of his Early Massachusetts Marriages. One volume of the Court Records at Plymouth, however, seems to have escaped his notice. It is an unnumbered volume of the Records of the Court of General Sessions of the Peace, and contains records of marriages for the years 1723 to 1737, none of which are found in Mr. Bailey's volume.

The purpose of issuing this pamphlet now is to supply such of Mr. Bailey's subscribers, as do not have a set of THE GENEALOGICAL ADVERTISER, with that portion of the Plymouth County Marriages contained in the unnumbered volume but not printed in his book. These occupy pages three to nineteen of this pamphlet. As this is intended for a supplement to his work, it is not thought necessary to index it. Scanning the pages for the name wanted is only a step beyond scanning the pages of an index in which the arrangement of names seems to have been determined by chance, Trask being the first name found under its initial and Thurston the last.

CAMBRIDGE, October, 1900.

The Genealogical Advertiser.

A QUARTERLY MAGAZINE OF FAMILY HISTORY, PUBLISHED IN MARCH, JUNE, SEPTEMBER AND DECEMBER.

EACH VOLUME CONTAINS ABOUT 165 OCTAVO PAGES AND IS THOROUGHLY INDEXED.

Subscription for the Current Year, $1.00.
Price of each completed volume, $1.50 in numbers, $2.00 bound.
Strictly net and payable in advance.

This magazine is devoted almost entirely to the publication of hitherto unprinted original records.

PRINCIPAL CONTENTS OF VOLUMES ONE, TWO AND THREE, 1898, 1899, AND 1900:

Abstracts of Bristol County, Mass., Probate Records.
Abstracts of Plymouth County, Mass., Probate Records.
Papers from Essex County, Mass., Records.
Papers from Middlesex County, Mass., Court Files.
Plymouth County, Mass., Marriages.
Bristol, Maine, Marriages.
Bristol, Maine, Genealogies.
Falmouth, Mass., Births, Marriages and Deaths.
Kingston, Mass., Births, Marriages and Deaths.
Pembroke, Mass., Births, Marriages and Deaths.
Sandwich, Mass., Births, Marriages and Deaths.
Stow, Mass., Epitaphs.
East Yarmouth, Mass., (now Dennis) Church Records, Admissions and Baptisms.
Weymouth, Mass., Church Records, Baptisms and Marriages.
Biographical sketch of Hon. Peter Bulkeley, M.A., 1641–1688. With portrait.
Biographical sketch of John Ward Dean, A.M. With portrait.
Biographical sketch of Rev. David Hall, D.D., of Sutton, 1704–1789. With portraits.
Descendants of William Cox, of Pemaquid.
United States Direct Tax, 1798, for Bristol and Waldoboro, Me.
Notes, Queries, Answers to Queries and Book Notes.

LUCY HALL GREENLAW, Publisher,
CAMBRIDGE, MASS.

PLYMOUTH COUNTY MARRIAGES.

FROM THE FIRST VOLUME OF THE RECORDS OF THE

INFERIOR COURT OF COMMON PLEAS,

AT PLYMOUTH, MASS.

---

[1] 1693 Registry of marriages within ye Town of Plimouth

John Dotey junr And mehetabel Nelson were married ffebruary ye 2d : 1692-3

Joseph ffinney of plimouth marryed to mary Bryant of ye same june 14th 1693 :

John Nelson of plimouth marryed to patience Morton of ye same may 4th 1693 :

Joseph Bucland was married to Deborah Barrow, October 17th 1693.

Jodathon Robbins & Hannah Pratt were marryed ye 11th day of January 1693-4

Saml Dunham senr & Sarah Watson Widdow was marryed ye 15th day of January 1693-4

Hugh Cole senr & mary morton Widdow were marryed ye 30th of January 1693-4

1694 John Dotey senr and Sarah Jones were married the 22d of Novembr 1694 :

George Barrow & patience Simmons were married the 14th of ffebruary 1694-5

Wm Little & Hannah w [not finished, entry erased.]

[2 Blank.]

[3] 1693 Registry of marriages within ye Town of Duxborough

James Thomas and mary Tilden were married January ye 3d 1692-3

Richard Waste and Mary Samson were marryed Octobr 26th 1693

James Soul was marryed to Lidia Tomson Decembr 14th : 1693

1

1694 Samuel Hill married to phebe Leonard Novembr 6th 1694

Elisha Wadsworth married to Elizabeth Wisewall ye 9th day of December 1694 :

1695 Saml Samson and Assadiah Eedey were marryed ye 29th day of may 1695

James Bonney and Abigail Bishop were married the 14th day of June 1695

[4 Blank]

[5] 1693   Registry of marriages within ye Town of Scituate

John Dwelley and Rachell Buck were married January ye 4th : 1692-3

Robert Stetson (son of Joseph Stetson) and mary callomer were married ye 12th of January 1692-3

Samuel Stodder and Elizabeth   were married ye 1st of march 1692-3

John Buck of Scituate married to Sarah Dotey of plimouth Aprill 26th 1693

[6 & 7 Blank]

[8] 1693   Registry of marriages within ye Town of marshfield

Thomas Tilden junr married to Hannah mendall the 20th day of December 1692 :

[9] Registry of maryages within ye Township of Bridgwater   1694 :

James Harris and Elizabeth Bayley both of bridgwater marryed ffebry 14th 1692-3

Richard Holt & Lidia wormwood of Bridgwater marryed may ye 10th 1693

James Washbourn & mary Bowden of Bridgwater marryed December ye 20th 1693 :

John Whitemore and Ruth Bassett were marryed ye 22d of Decembr 1692

Benjamin Snow and Elizabeth Alden were marryed the 12th of December 1693

John Emerson and Elizabeth Leech were married ye 27th of December 1693 :

[10 Blank]

[11]   Registry of marriages within the Township of Middleborough

1693 : James Wood Marryed to Experience ffuller Aprill 12th 1693

Jacob Tomson married to Abigail Wadsworth Decembr 28th : 1693

1694 Samuel Eaton and Elizabeth ffuller were married ye 24th of May 1694.

FROM THE UNNUMBERED* VOLUME OF THE COURT OF GENERAL SESSIONS OF THE PEACE.

[124] Marriages in the Town of Middleborough.

1729 March 27th Josiah Haskell and Sarah Brayley both of the Town of Middleborough—

April the 9th Joseph Leonard and Hannah Pratt both of the Town of Middleborough—

August 21st William Hack of Taunton and Mary Tinkham of Middleborough—

September 10th Eleazer Pratt Junr and Hannah Short both of Middleborough—

September 10th Joshua Combs of Rochester and Elizabeth Pratt of Middleborough—

November 20th Joshua Peirce of Pembroke and Hopestill Holloway of Middleborough—

December 25th Nathan Holloway of Taunton and Elizabeth makepeace of Middleborough—

By the Revd Benjamin Ruggles.

1728—May 24th Mr Seth Howland and Elizabeth Delano both of Middleborough—

September 10th Ebenezer Redden and Joanna Vaughan both of Middleborough—

October 31st David Miller and Susannah Holmes both of Middleborough—

December 4— Ignatius Elmes and Sarah Bennett both of Middleborough—

December 18 — Jonathan Snow of Bridgwater and Sarah Soul of Middleborough—

William Hooper of Bridgwater and Lois Thomas of Middleborough January 30th 1728

1729 April ultimo, Thomas Wood and Hannah Alden both of Middleborough—

---

*See Report on Custody and Condition of the Public Records of [Massachusetts] Parishes, Towns and Counties, page 354.

[125] May 15th Coombs Barrows and Joanna Smith both of Middleborough—

May 27— Robert Ransom and Sarah Chyles both of Middleborough—

July 17— John Savery Junr and Mary Thomas Daughter of Jonathan Thomas deceased both of the Town of Middleborough—

July ult : John Eaton of Kingston and Elizabeth Fuller of Middleborough—

December 11th The Rev.d Mr. John Wadsworth of Canterbury and Mrs. Abigail Sprout of Middleborough—

December 17— Jonathan Fuller and Hannah Harlow both of Middleborough—

December 23 — Captain Ichabod Tupper and Hananh Tinkham both of the Town of Middleborough—

1729-30 March 5th Deacon Thomas Pratt of Easton and Desire Bonney of Middleborough—

March 5th Isaac Billington and Mary Donham both of Middleborough—

1730 March 12th Robert Barrows and Fear Thomas both of Middleborough —

April 1st Peter Tinkham and Eunice Thomas both of Middleborough —

By the Revd. Peter Thatcher

A true Copy Transcribed from Middleborough Town Book Attest Jacob Tomson *Town Clerk.*

1730 — September 16. 1730 — Benjamin Leonard and Elizabeth West both of Middleborough—

1731—April 1st Electious Reynolds Junr and Charity Caswell both of the Town of Middleborough—

By   Benja Ruggles

1730 July 10th Francis Gayward of Rochester and Anna Morse Junr of Middleborough—

August 7th Mr Samuel Wood and the Widow Sarah Howland both of Middleborough—

November 12th Josiah Hatch of Pembroke and Mercy Redding of Middleborough—

[126] January 7th Mr. Jacob Tomson and Mrs. Elizabeth Holmes both of Middleborough—

February 18th John Wood and Hannah Chiles both of Middleborough—

1731 — March 31 — Mr Jacob Soul and Miss Mary Thomas both of Middleborough—

April 1—Thomas Holmes and Mary Sprout both of Middleborough—

November 22ᵈ Mʳ Francis Miller and miss Experience Sprout
both of Middleborough—

Decʳ 14—Obadiah Sampson and Mary Soul both of Middleborough—

February 17ᵗʰ Elias Miller and Sarah Holmes both of Middleborough—

1732 April 12—Thomas King and Mary Gaunt[?] both of
Middleborough—

April 25—Mʳ Thomas Tomson and miss Martha Soul both of
Middleborough—

June 26—John Miller Junr—and Watistill Clap both of Middleborough—

August 24—Mʳ Isaac Bennett and miss Mary Drew both of
Middleborough—

December 7ᵗʰ James Winslow a Seafaring Resident of Plymouth
and Susanna Conant of Middleborough—

January 4—Jesse Griffeth and Elizabeth Bent both of Middleborough

February 5ᵗʰ Samuel Eddy Junʳ and Lydia Alden both of Middleborough—

February 21ˢᵗ Mʳ Ebenezer Reed of Abington and miss Hannah Tompson of Middleborô.

February 22—Noah Thomas and Mary Alden both of Middleborough
By the Revᵈ Peter Thatcher

1733 May 10ᵗʰ Stephen Donham of Middleborough and
Lydia Taylor of Taunton--

[127] June 20—Nathaniel Holloway of the Town of Middleborough and Mehetabel Bassit of Bridgwater—
By Benjᵃ Ruggles

March 1732-3—James Bumpas and Rachel Hanks both of the
Town of Middleborough—

April 1733—Benjamin Wood and Presulla Rickard both of the
Town of Plimpton

Francis Eaton and Lydia Fuller both of the Town of Middleborough June 12ᵗʰ 1733—

November 1ˢᵗ 1733 Zacheriah Whitman of Bridgwater and
Eleanor Bennet of Middleborough
By Benjᵃ White Justice of Peace.

A true Copy Transcribed from Middleborough Town Book
—Attest Jacob Tomson *Town Clerk*

1731   Samuel Shaw of Plimpton and Desire Southworth
of Middleborough April 21st 1731- ·

June 14—— Benjamin Gurney and Sarah Morse both of Middle-
borough-—

January 16— Elkanah Sherman of Dartmouth and Margaret
Pitts of Middleborough—

1732   May 29—Combs Barrows and Mary Dwelly both of
Middleborough—

June 9th Samuel Thomas and Lydia Richmond both of Middleborough——

Nov' 2d Nathaniel Richmond of Taunton and Alice Hacket of
Middleborough—-and also Thomas Ramsdale and Mary
Peirce both of Middleborough—

    By   Benja Ruggles

1732   June 27—Eleazer Lyon and Bethiah Allen both of
Middleborough   By Benja White Just : of Peace

January 11th Jotham Caswell and Mary Renolds both of the
Town of Middleborough—

January 31st Timothy Rogers of Middleborough and Damaras
Macumber of Taunton
        By the Revd Benja Ruggles—

A true Copy Transcribed from Middleborough Town Book
Att. Jacob Tomson *Town Clerk*

[128]   Marriages in the Town of Plymouth—

1726-7   February 16—The Reverend Mr Robert Ward of
Wenham and miss Margaret Rogers of Plymouth—

March 16—Barnabas Shurtleff of Plimpton and Jemima
Adams—

1727—April 4—Joseph Bartlett and Sarah Morton both of
Plymouth—

April 17—Samuel Totman and Experience Rogers both of
Plymouth—

December 14—Ebenezer Cobb Junr and Lydia Stephens both
of Plymouth—

December 22—Benjamin Lothrop Junr of Barnstable and Experience Howland of Plymouth—

February 8th Ebenezer Cobb of Plymouth and Mary Thomas of
Middleborough—

    The above Marriages were solemnized by the Reverend
    Nathl Leonard—

1727 April 10—Samuel Doty and Marcy Cobb both of Plymouth—

September 28th Joshua Finney and Hannah Curtis both of Plymouth—

The above two Marriages were Solemnized by Isaac Lothrop Esq—

1728 June 6—Nehemiah Ripley and Sarah Atwood both of Plymouth—

August 6th Thomas Scarret and Alse Ward both of Plymouth—

October 28th Jo a Negro Man belonging to Mr Nathaniel Thomas and Phebe a Negro Woman belonging to Mr Haviland Torrey—

October 31—Elkanah Delano and Mary Sanders both of Plymouth—

November 14—Ephraim Sampson of Duxborough and Ruth Shepherd of Plymouth—

November 14—Samuel Cole and Mercy Barnes both of Plymouth—

December 12th Timothy Burbank of Boston now residing in Plymouth and Mary Kempton of Plymouth—

[129] December 19—Jonathan Freeman of Plimpton and Sarah Rider of Plymouth—

December 20—Thorton Gray and Katherine White both of Plymouth—

January 30—James Holmes and Content Silvester both of Plymouth—

February 18—Matthew Lemote and Mercy Billington both of Plymouth—

By the Reverd Nathl Leonard—

A true Copy Transcribed from the Records of the Town of Plymouth—Attest John Dryer *Town Clerk*

1729 April 3d Edward Stevens and Marcy Silvester both of Plymouth—

April 3d Rodolphus Hatch of Province Town and Esther Holmes of Plymouth—

May 20—Thomas Doane of Chatham and Sarah Barnes of Plymouth—

May 30—Thomas Totman and Lucretia Ross both of Plymouth—

June 30th Jack and Mariah Negroes belonging to Mr Jonathan Bryant—

July 8—Jacob Lewis and Bathsheba Mallis both of Plymouth—

July 8th John Watson Esqr and Mrs Priscilla Thomas both of Plymouth—

July 14—Jacob Taylor of Barnstable and Mary Atwood of Plymouth—

September 9th Seth Doggett and Elizabeth Delano both of Plymouth—

October 28—Isaac King and Hannah Harlow both of Plymouth—

November 20—John Cushing Esqr of Scituate and Miss Mary Cotton of Plymouth—

February 10—John Hambleton and Elizabeth Jones both of Plymouth—

March 4—Thomas Ward and Joanna Donham both of Plymouth

[130] 1730 March 27—Ephraim Churchill and Priscilla Manchester both of Plymouth—

May 4—Thomas Weston and Prudence Conant both of Plymouth

May 18—Mr William Dyre of Boston and Miss Hannah Phillips of Plymouth—

June 8—Deacon John Atwood and miss Experience Pierce both of Plymouth—

August 10th Nicholas Drew and Lydia Doggett both of Plymouth—

September 22—Ebenezer Finney of Barnstable and Rebecca Barnes of Plymouth—

September 24—John Studley and Elizabeth Doten both of Plymouth—

September 30—Jabez Holmes and Rebecca Harlow both of Plymouth—

The Foregoing Marriages were Solemnized by the Revd Nathl Leonard—

A true Copy Transcribed from the Records of the Town of Plymouth—

Marriages in the Town of Rochester—

1729 June 24—Nicholas Hicks and Hannah Coombs both of Rochester—

June 27—Stephen Ellis and Ruth Turner both of Rochester—

October 23d Seth Winslow and Abigail Whiteridge both of Rochester—

November 29—Jonathan Hunter and Hopestill Hamblin both of Rochester—

December 10—Archelaus Hammond and Elizabeth Weeks both of Rochester—

January 25th Nathaniel Parker of Rochester and Sarah Parker of Dartmouth—

[131] February 19th George Barlow and Ruth Barrow both of Rochester were married—

February 26 — Seth Ellis and Mary Bumpas both of Rochester were married—

1730 April 16 — James Steward and Hannah Dexter both of Rochester were married—

November 5th Samuel Hammond and Deliverance Admister both of Rochester—

November 12th Benjamin Hammond And Priscilla Sprague both of Rochester—

December 8th Lowis Deneranville and Susanna Crapo both of Rochester—

December 31 — Ebenezer Keen and Mercy Whiteridge both of Rochester were married—

March 1st Stephen Goodspeed and Bethiah Wooding both of Rochester

The foregoing Marriages were Solemnized by the Reverend Timothy Ruggles—

1726 November 17th Edward Doty and Mary Andrews both of Rochester were married—

November 23 — Seth ORiley of Yarmouth and Mehitabel Wing of Rochester—

February 28th John Grass and Penelope White both of Rochester were married—

1727 April 15th James Pratt and Frances Combs both of Rochester were married—

1728 January 1st Joseph Ashely and Mary Whetredge both of Rochester were married—

1729 July 10th James Foster and Lydia Winslow both of Rochester—

1730 June 18 — Abiel Sprague and Elizabeth Ashely both of Rochester—

October 10th Chillingsworth Foster of Harwich and Marcy Winslow of Rochester—

November 19th Benjamin Cole of Swansey and Elizabeth Nelson of Middleborough—

The above Marriages were Solemnized by Edward Winslow Justice of the Peace—

A true Copy of all the Marriages that have been to me Returned S Wing T *Clerk*

[132] 1731 May 31st James Whitcomb and Sarah Link-horn both of Rochester were married—

June 22 — John Ross and Sarah Clifton both of Rochester were married—

August 22 — Micah Sprague and Elizabeth Turner both of Rochester—

October 13 — Ebenezer Lothrop of Mansfield and Elizabeth Hammond of Rochester—

October 21 — Hinkman Vaughan of Middleborough and Desire Hicks of Rochester—

November 4 — Ithamas Comes and Hannah Andrews both of Rochester—

January 13 — Robert Whitcomb and Joanna Lawrance both of Rochester—

1732 May 18 — Samuel Dexter and Mary Clark both of Rochester

July 23 — Joseph Barlow and Abigail Wyatt both of Rochester—

September 25 — Barnabas Sears and Thankful Freeman both of Rochester—

October 6 — Benjamin Clap and Katherine Nye both of Rochester—

December 21st Josiah Bump and Hannah Bump both of Rochester—

January 5th Cornelius Connor and Hitte Haskell both of Rochester—

By the Revend Timothy Ruggles

1733 October 18 — Ebenezer Luce and Sarah Doty both of Rochester—

October 17 — Jedidiah Briggs and Jedida Ellis both of Rochester were married—

October 25 — David Nye and Elizabeth Briggs both of Rochester—

November 22 — Abraham Ashley and Elizabeth Rogers both of Rochester—

November 25 — Barzillai Randall and Jerusha Hammond both of Rochester—

November 25th Thomas Whetredge and Hannah Haskell both of Rochester—

November 25th Andrew Haskell and Jane Clark both of Rochester—

[133] December 31 — Jonathan Spooner and Mary Crapoo both of Rochester were married—

March 14 — Samuel White and Elizabeth Ashley both of Rochester—

1732 — May 28 — William Randall Junr and Rest Sumer both of Rochester—

September 18 — Nathaniel Chabbuch Junr and Tabitha Besse Agawam Plymouth—

January 11 — Caleb Benson of Middleborough and Deborah Barrow of Plympton—

February 12 — William Ashley and Elizabeth Ashley both of Rochester—

1733 August 16 — Samuel Edward and Rebeckah Burge both of Rochester—

October 18 — Ebenezer Luce and Sarah Doty both of Rochester—

October 19 — Jedidiah Briggs and Jedidah Ellis both of Rochester—

October 25 — David Nye and Elizabeth Briggs

November 22 — Abraham Ashley and Elizabeth Rogers both of Rochester

November 25 — Barzillai Randall and Jerusha Hammond both of Rochester—

November 25 — Thomas Wetteridge and Hannah Haskell both of Rochester—

Novr 25 — Andrew Haskell and Jane Clark both of Rochester—

December 31 — Jonathan Spooner and Mary Crapoo both of Rochester—

March 14 — Samuel White and Elizabeth Ashley both of Rochester—

1734 October 31 — James Lake of Dartmouth and Elizabeth Crapoo of Rochester—

1737 — October 13th Samuel Bumpas and Abigail Bumpas both of Rochester—

October 19 — Isaac Doty and Elizabeth Blackmer both of Rochester—

October 20 — Samuel Robinson and Elizabeth Doty both of Rochester—

November 22d John Barrows and Joanna Dexter both of Rochester—

February 16 — Ebenezer Briggs and Betta Gibbs both of Rochester—

By the Revd Timothy Ruggles—

Copy examined pr Noah Sprague T *Clerk*—

[134]   Hanover Marriages.

1728   January 16 — David Bryant Junr of Scituate and Hannah Turner of Hanover—

February 20 — Richard Hill and Jemimah Ramsdil both of Hanover—

1729   May 15 — Benjamin Barstow and Sarah Bardin both of Hanover—

July 7 — Jonathan Potter and Margaret Frank both of Hanover—

October 9th   Ezekiel Palmer and Martha Pratt both of Hanover—

1730   April 23 — Joseph Ramsdell and Mary Homer both of Hanover—

June 15th   Clemond Bate and Agatha Meritt both of Hanover—

Sept 24 — Matthew Stetson of Hanover and Hannah Lincoln of Scituate—

February 18 — Melatiah Dillingham and Phebe Hatch both of Hanover—

1731   April 22d   John Low of Pembroke and Susanna Gilford of Hanover —

May 12 — Eliab Turner and Martha Barstow both of Hanover—

June 4th   Isaac Barden and Deborah Tobey both of Hanover—

August 4th   Richard Bowker and Sarah Palmer both of Hanover—

By the Revd Benjamin Bass—

A true Copy of the Records of Hanover Exam^d p^r William Withrell Town *Clerk*

[135]   Marriages Solemnized in the Town of Bridgwater—

1726   November 15th   Field and Mary Haward both of Bridgwater were married—

November 29 —   Whitman and Elizabeth Rickard both of Bridgwater were married—

By the Revd Daniel Perkins

1724 — April 8 — Solomon Snow and Bathsheba Mahurin both of Bridgwater —

May 13 — Joseph Byram and Martha Perkins both of Bridgwater—

1725 — October 21 — Zacheus Packard and Mercy Allden both of Bridgwater—

December 17 — Hugh Mahurin and Mary Snell both of Bridgwater—

May 4th   Joseph Carver and Elizabeth Snow both of Bridgwater—

May the 5th Stephen Leach and Sarah Hooper both of Bridgwater—

1726 — November 17th Samuel Phillips and Lydia Bassett both of Bridgwater—

1727—Joseph Drake and Alice Hayward both of Bridgwater — April 5th

April 6 — Elisha Dunbar and Mercy Hayward both of Bridgwater—

By Josiah Edson Justice of Peace—

1726 Novr 24 — Henry Kingman and Mary Allen both of Bridgwater —

January 17 — Recompense Cary and the Widow Sarah Brett—

By the Revd John Angier—

1728 January 23d Josiah Snell and Abigail Fobes both of Bridgwater—

1729 — June the 10th John Wormal and Mary Bryant both of Bridgewater—

July 22d Samuel Packard and Susanna Kinsley both of Bridgwater—

August 6 — Benjamin Washburn and Martha Kingman both of Bridgwater—

October 17 — Joseph Perry and Mary Chandler both of Bridgwater—

December 22d Nathl Davenport and Lucy Wyeman both of Bridgwater—

December 9th Ephraim Dunham and Elizabeth Bump both of Bridgwater—

By the Revd Daniel Perkins

[136] October 15th Christopher Askins and Susanna Robinson both of Bridgwater—

November 10 th John Whitman and Elizabeth Cary both of Bridgwater—

November 13 — Caleb Brand and Damaras James both of Bridgwater—

December 30 — Samuel Pratt and Bithia Byram both of Bridgwater—

January 7th — Benjamin Allen and Mehitebel Cary both of Bridgwater—

January 28 — Zachariah Whitmarsh and Hannah Washburn both of Bridgwater—

1730 — April 16th Davenport and Sarah Richards both of Bridgwater—

November 12th Timothy Hayward and Mary Reed both of
Bridgwater—
November 12th Arthur Harris and Mehitabel Rickard both of
Bridgwater—
1731   October 21st John Johnson and Peggy Holman both
of Bridgwater—
        By the Revd John Angier—
1730 — January 1st Jacob Allen and Abigail Kingman both
of Bridgwater—
January 13 — Isaac Kingman and Jane Kingman both of
Bridgewater—
March 23 — Joseph Davis and Ruth Bassett both of Bridg-
water --
        By the Revd Daniel *Perkins*
1729 — October 15th Christopher Askins and Susanna
Robinson were married — both of Bridgwater—
November 10 — John Whitman and Elizabeth Cary both of
Bridgwater—
November 13 -- Caleb Brand and Damaris James both of Bridg-
water—
December 30 — Samuel Pratt and Bethiah Byram both of
Bridgwater—
January 7th Benjamin Allen and Mehitabel Cary both of Bridg-
water—
        [137] January 28 — Zachary Whitmarsh and Hannah
Washburn both of Bridgwater were married—
1730 — April 16 --- William Davenport and Sarah Richards
both of Bridgwater—
        By the Revd John Angier—
1730 — November 12th Timothy Hayward and the Widow
Mary Reed both of Bridgwater—
November 12 — Arthur Harris and Mehetable Rickard both of
Bridgwater—
1731 — October 21st John Johnson and Pegge Holman both
of Bridgwater—
1730 — October 14 — Shubal Waldow and Abagail Allen
both of Bridgwater—
March 11 — David Snow and Joanna Hayward both of Bridgwater—
March 11 — Zachariah Snell and Abigail Hayward both of
Bridgwater—

1731 June 20th Thomas Ames and Keziah Hayward both of Bridgwater—

June 23 — Samuel Soper and Esther Littlefield both of Bridgwater—

June 24 — Israel Alger and Rachel Wade both of Bridgwater—

July 11th John Snow and Hannah Hayward both of Bridgwater—

July 29 — Wright Bartlett and Bethia Packard both of Bridgwater—

March 1st 1731 — David Kingman and Mercy Hayward both of Bridgwater—

March 1st Jonathan Kingman and Mercy Keith both of Bridgwater—

By the Revd Daniel *Perkins*—

1732 — November 24th William Gillemer and Mary Willis both of Bridgwater—

1731 — November 25 — Jonathan Alden of Marshfield and Mehetable Allen of Bridgwater—

December 23 Benjamin Mahurin and Lydia Pratt both of Bridgwater—

January 13 — Solomon Washburn and Martha Orcutt both of Bridgwater—

[138] February 8th Benjamin Johnson and Ruth Holman both of Bridgwater—

February 24 — Mr Shepherd Fisk and miss Alice Alger both of Bridgwater—

1732 — June 15th Joseph Cary and Anna Brett both of Bridgwater—

By the Revd John Shaw—

1732 — May 17 — John Randall and Experience Willis both of Bridgwater—

May 15th William Brett and Bethiah Kingsly both of Bridgwater—

May 25 — Benjamin Curtis and Experience Hayward both of Bridgwater—

August 14 — Isaac Willis and Hannah Pratt both of Bridgwater—

September 21 — Mr Ephraim Keith and Miss Sarah Washburn both of Bridgwater —

October 21th Joseph Gannett and Hannah Brett both of Bridgwater—

By the Revd Daniel *Perkins*—

Duxborough Marriages

1726 — January 3ᵈ David Seabury now resident in Duxborough and Abigail Seabury of Duxborough—

By the Revᵈ John Robinson—

1729 — September 25 — Abraham Pierce of Pembroke Junʳ and Abigail Peterson of Duxborough—

November 25 — Thomas Prince and Judea Fox both of Duxborough —

December 19 — Joseph Trebble and Anna Jones both of Plymouth—

January 8ᵗʰ Amaziah Delano and Ruth Samson both of Duxborough—

March 2ᵈ Abner Weston and Sarah Standish both of Duxborough—

1730 — May 4ᵗʰ Ebenezer Sherman and Bathsheba Foord both of Marshfield —

August 5 — John Soul and Mabel Partridge both of Duxborough—

By Edward Arnold Justice of *Peace*

[139] October 8ᵗʰ Ebenezer Bartlett and Jerusha Samson both of Duxborough—

1731 — October 26 — Benjamin Simmons Junʳ and Fear Samson both of Duxborough—

1732 — July 6 — Reuben Peterson and Rebakah Simmons both of Duxborough—

July 27 — Ezra Arnold and Rebaca Sprague both of Duxborough—

October 24 — Isaac Simmons and Lydia Cushman both of Duxborough—

By Edward Arnold Justice of *Peace*

Marriages in the Town of Marshfield—

1723 — March 28 — Ebenezer Howland and Sarah Green both of Marshfield were married—

May 29 — James Dexter of Rochester and Lois Sherman of Marshfield—

June 3ᵈ Thomas Tracy and Susanna Waterman both of Marshfield---

October 31 — Benjamin Kent and Persis Doggett both of Marshfield---

January 7 — John Logan and Margaret Carr both of Marshfield—

January 30 — Joshua Rose and Elizabeth Gibson both of Marshfield—

January 30 — James Warren of Plymouth and Penelope Winslow of Marshfield—

February 17 — Samuel Sherman and Mary Williamson both of
Marshfield—

March 11 — Francis Crooker and Patience Childs both of Marshfield—

    1724—April 23 — Benjamin Hanks and Mary White both
of Marshfield —

May 23 — Joshua Samson and Mary Oakman both of Marshfield.

July 8th Thomas Stockbridge of Scituate and Hannah Rogers of
Marshfield

    [140] October 8 — Mr John Thomas and Miss Mary Ray
both of Marshfield—

October 21 — Caleb Oldham of Scituate and Bethiah Stephens
of Marshfield—

October 9th William Stephens and Patience Jones both of Marshfield—

February 23 — Thomas Phillips and Mary Sherman both of
Marshfield—

    1725 March 25 — Anthony Eames and Anna Barker both
of Marshfield—

June the 2d Ichabod Washburn of Plymouth and Bethiah Phillips of Marshfield—

October 21st William Lucas and Sarah Thomas both of Marshfield—

October 27th Israel Hatch of Scituate and Bethiah Thomas of
Marshfield—

October 27 — Nathaniel Keen of Pembroke and Thankful Winslow of Marshfield—

October 27 — Ebenezer Damon of Scituate and Abigail Thomas
of Marshfield—

October 7th William Hambelton and Jane Hopkins both of
Marshfield—

January 6th Adam Hall and Sarah Sherman both of Marshfield—

January 13 — Silvanus Hall of Plymouth and Elizabeth Doggett
of Marshfield—

February 16 — John Winslow of Plymouth and Mary Little of Marshfield —

1726 — May 26 — John Polan and Thankful Atkins both of Marshfield—.

September 14 — Josiah Phinney of Plymouth and Mercy Thomas of Marshfield—

Novembr 9th Samuel Baker and Hannah Foord both of Marshfield—

November 9th Seth Joyce and Rachel Sherman both of Marshfield—

1727 April 5th John Deyre and Mary Trouant both of Marshfield—

[141] May 8th Thomas Oldham of Scituate and Desire Wormall of Marshfield—

June 18 — Robert Waterman of Plimpton and Abigail Dingley of Marshfield—

January 11 —Ebenezer Taylor and Sarah Carver both of Marshfield—

January 24 — Stephen Stoddard of Hingham and Rebecca King of Marshfield

January 25 — Isaac Phillips and Sarah White both of Marshfield

March 19 — Ebenezer Jones and Jane King both of Marshfield—

March 19 — Bezaliel Palmer of Scituate and Anna Jones of Marshfield—

1728 — May 28 — Isaac Taylor of Pembroke and Jerusha Tilden of Marshfield—

July 4 — Joshua Carver and Martha Foord both of Marshfield—

October 14 — Tobias Payne of Boston and Sarah Winslow of Marshfield —

October 30 — William Foord and Hannah Barstow both of Marshfield —

November 6 — Snow Winslow and Deborah Bryant both of Marshfield —

November 14 — Samuel Kent and Desire Barker both of Marshfield—

November 28 — John Magoun of Scituate and Abigail Waterman of Marshfield —

December 11 — Thomas Doggett and Joannah Fuller both of Marshfield—

December 19 — Joseph Hewitt and Sarah Dingley both of Marshfield—

January 18 — Benjamin Phillips and Desire Sherman both of Marshfield—

January 18 — Joshua Eames and Abigail Doggett both of Marshfield—

January 16 — Samuel Foord and Sarah Rogers both of Marshfield—

1724 December 11th Anthony Eames and Grace Oldham
of Scituate—

The Forgoing Marriages were Solemnized by the Revd.
Mr Gardner—

FROM VOLUME ONE OF THE COURT OF GENERAL SESSIONS OF
THE PEACE.

[101] Duxborough Marriages from 1734 To 1737,

Robert Samson and Else Samson both of Duxborough were
Maried December the 19. 1734.

Hartale Jaffere & Betty Tom both of Plymouth were Maried
December 23. 1734.

John Wadsworth Junr. and Mary Allden both of Duxborough
were Maried December 31. 1734.
pr. Edward Arnold Just peace.

[102] Duxborough Mariages.

Nathaniel Phillips and Joanna White both of Marshfield were
Maried Jany 16. 1734.

James Arnold & Joannah Sprague both of Duxborough were
maried February 19. 1734.

Ichabod Brewster of Duxborough & Lidiah Barstow of Pembroke were Maried June 3. 1735.

Seth Bartlet & Charity Cullifer both of Duxborough were maried
the 27th of February A. D. 1735-6.
The aforesd persons were Maried pr. Edw Arnold Just
peace

Nathaniel Dunham of Plymouth & Anne Peterson of Duxborough
were Maried at Duxborough April 7. 1735   pr. John
Robinson.

Joseph Morgan of Preston in the Colony of Conneticut & Ruth
Brewster of Duxborough were maried at Duxborough May
8. 1735.   pr John Robinson Clerk.

John Pryer & Mercy Dellano both of Duxborough were maried
in Duxborough Oct. 14. 1735.   pr. me John Robinson.

Mr Joanathan Trumble of Lebanon in the Collony of Conneticut
& mrs Faith Robinson of Duxborough were maried at Duxboro. Decemr. 9. 1735   pr me Jno. Robinson

Ichabod Wadsworth Junr. & Anne Hunt both of Duxborough
were maied in Duxborough November 25. 1736.   pr John
Robinson Clerk.

Asa Hunt and Sarah Partridge both of Duxborough were maried at Duxborough December 2d. 1736.
       pr John Robinson Clerk.

Ichabod Wormwell and Lydia Dellano both of Duxboro were Maried at Duxborough December 13, 1736.   pr John Robinson Clerk. .

Samuel Drew Junr. of Kingston and Anne White of Duxborough were maried at Duxborough December 28. 1736   pr Jno. Robinson Clerk

Sylvanus Curtiss of Plymouth and Dorothy Dellano of Duxboro were Maried at Duxborough November 26, 1734   pr me John Robinson

John Hanks and Mary Delano both of Duxborough were Maried in Duxboro January 16. 1734–5   pr me Jno. Robinson

Allerton Cushman of Plymton & Allathea Sole of Duxborough were Maried in Duxborough January 30. 1734–5   pr me Jno. Robinson

Samuel Wormwel and Mary Forest 17 January 1736–7.

May 11. Isaac Simmons & Elizabeth Sams.

Seth Bartlet & Martha Bourn 23d. November.

Experience Holmes of Dartmouth & Hannah Samson of Rochester maried December 13. 1737.

Caleb Jenney of Dartmouth & Patience Standish of Duxborough maried April 6. 1738

    [103]   Rochester Mariages.

1. Samuel Ruggles & Allis Sherman were Maryed June 25. 1738.
2. Josiah Jenkins of Barnstable & Mary Ellis of Rochester Maryed July 6. 1738.
3. Joseph Edwards Junr. & Sarah Burge were Maried July 13. 1738.
4. David Bessey Junr. & Dinah Maxum were Maryed July 20. 1738.
5. Nathaniel Whitcomb & Phœbe Blackmer maried July 27. 1738.
6. Uriah Savory & Deborah Bumpass were maried September 3. 1738.
7. Nathan Bumpas & Lydia Bumpas were maried October 19. 1738.
8. Zaccheus Bumpas & Reliance Morey were maried October 19. 1738.
9. Samuel Hix of Dartmouth & Ruth Hoskens of Rochr. maried Janry. 9. 1738–9.

10. Samuel Doty & Zerviah Lovel were Maried Jany. 18. 1738-9.

By me Timothy Ruggles.

Recorded in Rr. Town Book pr. Noah Sprague T. Cler

[112] Mariages in the Town of Pembrooke From 1724. To 1738.

Jacob Ellis of Herwich & Elizabeth Foster of Pembrooke were maried August 20. 1724.

Ichabod Bonney & Elisa. Howland 29th. October 1724.

Samuel Parris and Ruth Bonney Janry 21. 1725.

Isaac Sole & Egatha Parry March 11. 1725.

Josiah Foster Junr. & Mary Bonney July 29. 1725.

Thomas Holloway and Rebecca Tubs Septr. 14th. 1725.

John Mackfarland Junr. & Mary Foster March 28. 1726.

Benja. Hanks and Mary Ripley of Bridgwater March 23. 1727.

Nathn. Pearce and Keturah Newland April 27. 1727.

Mr. Jacob Norton of Chilmark & Mrs. Hannah Barker June 8. 1727.

Andrew Miller and Jane Macklucas December 19. 1727.

Joseph Stetson junr. & Abigail Hatch December 26. 1727.

Ezekiel Turner of Scituate & Batheba Stockbridge December 27. 1727.

Joseph Parry & Rebecca Joslyn both of Hanover April 24. 1728.

Thomas Partin & Margrett Gorden May 30. 1728.

John Franckley of Rehoboth & Hannah Record October 16. 1728.

John Lambert Junr. & Sarah Staples both of Hanover Novr. 4. 1728.

Anthony Winslow of Marshfield and Deborah Barker June 7. 1729.

Ebenr. Bonney & Elisa. Parriss Octo. 16 1729.

Joseph Chandler & Deborah Bonney Novr. 27. 1729.

Rouse Howland & Ann Bonney Novr. 27: 1729.

Elisha Bonney & Elisa. Lincoln Decr. 10. 1729.

Joseph Tubs junr. & Eliza. Randall Decr. 11. 1729.

James Hayes & Abigail Knapp Febyr, 25. 1730.

Joshua Baker & Sarah Cushing Septr. 3 1730.

Lott Thacher of Barnstable & Rebecca Keen Septr. 29. 1730.

Benja. Thomas of Marsfield & Gennet Stetson Novr. 5. 1730.

Solo. Beals junr. & Ann Howland Novr. 10. 1730.

Isaac Wadsworth & Susanna Nichols Decr. 16. 1730.

Joshua Turner & Sarah Winslow of Scituate Janry. 28. 1731.

Abraham Howland junr. & Sarah Simmons of Plympton March 11, 1731.

Zechariah Simmons of Duxboro. & Deborah Bishop May 27. 1731.

Nicholas Webster & Content Bishop Septr. 7. 1731.

Nehl. Pearce and Eliza. Hanks Octo. 27. 1731.

Isaac Oldham junr. & Mary Stetson Novr. 11. 1731.

Isaac Mackfarland & Sarah Foster Decr. 8. 1731.

Isaac Foster & Francees Joslyn of Hanover Janry. 6. 1732.

Thomas Elmour of Hanover and Elisa. Russell Mar. 16. 1732.

Barnas. Perry & Alce Sole of Duxboro. Mar. 30. 1732.

[113] Isaac Little Esqr and Mrs. Abigail Thomas Novr. 29. 1732.

George Russel and Hannah Mackfarland Decr. 18. 1732.

Andrew Linsey & Jane Curbe April 5. 1723.

Job Bonney & Ruth Bisbe May 9. 1733.

Daniel Hayford & Deliverance Boles May 24. 1733.

Thomas Tracy & Lidia Barstow of Hanover May 28. 1733.

John Bisbe junr. & Abiah Bonney Septr. 6. 1733.

Jesse Foord & Mary Crooker Octo. 17. 1733.

Aaron Sole junr. & Lidia Peterson of Duxborough Decr. 26. 1733.

Thomas Hayford & Susanna Perry Septr. 23. 1734.

Samuel Parry & Unice Wethrel of Hanover Septr. 24. 1734.

William Mackfarland & Sarah Peterson of Duxboro. Novr. 18. 1734.

John Stetson & Abigail Crooker Novr. 28. 1734.

Ezekiel Bonney and Hannah Bryant Decr. 26. 1734.

Joseph Foord Junr. and Hannah Nichols Mar. 6 1735.

Joseph Stetson & the Widdow Mary Parry Mar. 1 1736.

Job Randall and Mary Jennings Mar. 4. 1736.

Danll. Crooker & Mary Ramsdell April 28. 1736.

Elijah Cushing and Hannah Barker of Hanover May 3. 1736.

Jedediah Lincoln of Hingham and the Widdow Mary Barker June 10. 1736.

Daniel Lewis Junr. & Sarah Bisbe Junr. Septr. 30. 1736.

Austin Bearse of Halifax and Hannah Stetson Octo. 21. 1736.

Joseph Osyer and Mercy Thomas Decr. 8. 1736.

By Elisha Bisbe Esqr.

Josiah Bishop and Sarah Crooker Decr. 16. 1736.

Samuel Keen & Margaret Reddin of Scituate Janry. 4. 1737.

Benjᵃ. Jacob of Scituate and Mary Thomas May 12. 1737.

James Randall & Ruth Magoon June 15. 1737.

Elijah Bonney & Susanna Tubbs June 27. 1737.

Deacon Joseph Foord and the Widdo Sarah Dogget of Marsh field Septʳ. 7. 1737.

Jedediah Beals & Deborah Boles April 5. 1738.

All but One Maried by the Reverᵈ. Mʳ. Daniel Lewis the 19ᵗʰ. of December 1737 all but the last, and Recorded pʳ. Thomas Burton   Town Clerk for Pembrooke.

Received Sept. 6. 1738 pʳ. Edward Winslow Cler.

[153]   A list of Middleboro. Mariages. from 1733.   To 1740. ———

May 10. 1733.   Then Stephen Donham of Middleboro. & Lydia Taylor of Taunton was maried by me ——— Benjᵃ. Ruggles ———

June 20. 1733   Then Nathˡˡ. Holloway of the Town of Middleboro. & Mehitable Bassett of Bridgewater was Maried by me— Benjᵃ. Ruggles———

James Bumpas & Rachell Hanks both of the Town of Middleboro. were maried March 14. 1732–3 By me, Benjᵃ. White Just peace.

Benjᵃ. Wood & Priscilla Rickard, both of the Town of Plymton were maried April 12. 1733.   By me Benjᵃ. White   Just Peace

Francis Eaton & Lydia Fuller both of the Town of Middleboro. were maried June the 12ᵗʰ 1733. by me
                    Benjᵃ White   Just of peace.

Middleboro. Novembʳ. 1ˢᵗ. 1733.   Then was maried at Middleboro. aforesᵈ. Zachry. Whitman of Bridgwater & Elinor Bennet of Middleboro.
                    pʳ. me Benjᵃ. White Just of peace

March 20. 1733–4 Then Ebenʳ. Hayford of Middleboro. & Mary Brooman of Taunton were maryed by me.   Benjᵃ. Ruggles

May 3. 1734 then Caleb Cowing of Rochester & Anna Richmond of Middleboro. was maried by me——
          Benjᵃ. Ruggles————————————————

[154]   July 4ᵗʰ. 1734.   Then William Smith & Elisabeth Renolds both of Middleboro. was maried by me—Benjᵃ Ruggles———

July 30. 1734   Then Ephraim Pratt of Seabrooke and Beulah Williamson of Middleboro. was maried by me—Benjᵃ. Ruggles.

Transcribed from Middleboro. **Town Book** by me. Jacob Tomson   Town Clerk

Novr. 7. 1734. then Benja. Waldron of Dighton & Hannah Hackett of Middleboro. was maried by me—— Benja. Ruggles.

Jany. 30. 1734–5 Then John Montgomery & Mary Strawbridge both of the Town of Middleboro. was maried by me
————————————————————Benja. Ruggles.

Middleboro. March 20. 1734–5 then was mared at Middleboro. aforesd.——Edmond Weston & Eliza. Smith both of Middleboro.————
pr me Benja White Just Peace.

Middleboro. June 19. 1735 Then was maried at Middleboro. aforesd. Thomas Tupper & Rebecca Bumpas both of Middleborough——
pr me Benja. White Just Peace

May 5th 1735. Then Isaac Peirce Junr. & Deliverance Hollaway both Middleboro. was Maried by me — Benja Ruggles—

Transcribed From Middleboro. Town Book by me Jacob Tomson   T Cler.

February 7th. 1733–4 Willm. Redding & Bennett Eddy both of Middleboro. after lawfull publication in presents of parents were maryed.   Peter Thacher

April 2. 1734. Nathan Cobb of Plymo. & Joanna Bennet of Middleboro. after lawfull publication & Consent of parents were maryed. by Peter Thacher

June 13. 1734. Saml. Warren junr. & Rebecca Donham both of Middleboro were maryed — by Peter Thacher

Augt. 6. 1734 Joseph Jennings & Hannah Thomas both of Middleboro. were maryed ——————— By Peter Thacher

Nov. 6. 1734. Ephraim Tompson of Hallifax & Joanna Thomas of Middleboro. were maryed —— by Peter Thacher——

Novr. 7. 1734. John Cannady & Anna Hathaway both of Middleboro. were maryed —— by Peter Thacher

Febry. 6. 1734–5 Nathll. Foster of Plymo. & Mercy Thacher of Middleboro. were maryed by their ffather ——
Peter Thacher

Mar 25. 1735 Moses Eddy & Jedediah Wood both of Middleboro, were maryed —— By Peter Thacher—— ——

Apr 23. 1735 Elnathan Wood & Patience Cushman both of Middleboro. were maryed —— by Peter Thacher

May 1 : 1735 Nathan Thomas & Abigail Allden both of Middleboro. were maryed —— by Peter Thacher

July 13. 1735 Silvanus Brimhorn of Plymoth & Mary Bennet of Middleboro. were maryed by——— Peter Thacher

Augt 12. 1735. Daniel Vaughn & Sarah Cushman both of Middleboro. were maryed———————by Peter Thacher

Augt. 19. 1735. John Jackson & Joanna Bate both of Middleboro. were maryed——————By Peter Thacher—

Septr. 11. 1735 Peter Bennet junr. & Sarah Stephens both of Middleboro. were maryed ——— By Peter Thacher——

Octo. 7. 1735. Hezekiah Purrington of Truro & Mercy Bate of Middleboro. were maryed by Peter Thacher———

[155] Octo. 30. 1735. John Miller & Priscilla Bennet both of Middlebor. were maryed by———Peter Thacher

Novr. 6. 1735. Simeon Leonard & Abigail Morss both of Middleboro. were maryed ——— by — Peter Thacher

Decr. 25. 1735. Willm. Cushman & Susanna Samson both of Middleboro were maryed————— By Peter Thacher———

Decr. 25. 1735 Wm. Cushman & Susanna Samson both of Middleboro. — were maryed ———By Peter Thacher

Transcribed from Middleboro. Town book. by me Jacob Tomson Town Clerk

Middleboro. Novr. 13. 1735. Then Nathll. Macomber of Taunton & Priscilla Southworth of Middleboro. was maryed by me — Benja. Ruggles ———

Mar. 10. 1737. Then Benja. Renolds & Sarah Smith both of Middleboro. were maryed by me. Benja Ruggles

May 12. 1737. Then Willm. Holloway of Midd.eboro. & Sarah Walker of Taunton were maryed by me ———
Benja Ruggles———————————————

Febry. 2. 1737-8 Then Robt. Sprout & Hannah Samson both of Middleboro. were maryed by me — Benja. Ruggles

May 1. 1738 Then Benja Samson junr. of Plymton & Mary Williamson of Middleboro. were maryed by me — Benja. Ruggles.

Septr. 30. 1738 Then Daniel Tayler junr. & Mary Russell both of Middleboro. were maryed — by me Benja. Ruggles ———

Novr. 2. 1738 Then George Williamson Junr. & Fear Eddy both of the Town of Middleboro. were maryed by me Benja. Ruggles

July 7th. 1737. Samuel Holloway & Rebecca Treuant both of Middleboro. was maried — by me Benja Ruggles —

4

Augt. 16. 1737. Shadrach Peirce of Middlebor^o. & Abigail Hoskins of Taunton was maried—by me Benj^a. Ruggles————

Oct^o. 25. 1737. James Keith of Bridgwater & Deborah Bennet of Middlebor^o. were maried — by me Benj^a Ruggles.

Novr. 17. 1737. Charles West & Deborah Williamson both of Middlebor^o. were maried — by me Benj^a Ruggles.

Janr^y. 6th. 1737-8 Phillip Leonard & Mary Richmond both of Middlebor^o. were maried —— by me Benj^a. Ruggles

Novr. 23. 1738. Then John Hayford of Fretown & Thankfull Finney of Middlebor^o. were maried by me — Benj^a Ruggles ————

Janr^y. 4 1738-9 Then Ephraim Keen of Fretown & Mercy Allen of Middlebor^o. were maryed — by me Benj^a Ruggles

Mar 2 1738-9 Then John Hodson & Sarah Renals both of Middlebor^o. were maryed by me———— Benj^a Ruggles

Augt. 16. 1739 Then Ephraim Renolds & Alice Braley both of Middlebor^o. were maryed — by me Benj^a Ruggles

Novr. 29. 1739 Then Josiah Holloway & Hannah Parris both of Middlebor^o. were maried by me – Benj^a. Ruggles.

[156] June 18. 1740. Then M^r. Mark Haskell of Rochester & M^{rs}. Abiah Nelson of Middlebor^o. were maryed by me. Benj^a Ruggles.

October 2. 1740 Then William Nelson & Eliz^a. Howland both of Middlebor^o. were maryed by me ———— Benj^a. Ruggles.

Janr^y. 29th. 1735-6 Then was maried at Middlebor^o. Josiah Woods & Mary Holmes both of s^d. Town
P^r. me Benj^a White Just peace

Febr^y. 20. 1735-6 Then was maried at Middlebor^o. John Smith & Deborah Bardin both of s^d. Town —
p^r me Benj^a White Just peace

July 27. 1737. Then was maried at Middlebor^o. John Warren & Ann Reed both of s^d. Town——p^{r}me Benj^a White Just peace

Septr. 6. 1737. Then was maried at Middlebor^o. Jon^a. Smith Junr. & Experience Cushman both of s^d. Town. p^r me Benj^a White Just Peace

January the 25th. 1738-9 Then was maried at Middlebor^o. Seth Howland & Lydia Cobb both of s^d. Town. p^r me Benj^a White Just peace.

May 4th. 1739. Then was maried at Middlebor^o. Nathan Caswell & Hannah Shaw both of Middlebor^o. p^r me Benj^a White Just peace

Febr^y. 28. 1739-40 then was maried at Middlebor^o. Gersham Cobb Junr. & Meriam Thomas, jun both of s^d. Town
p^r. me Benj^a White Just peace

Febrʸ. the 28ᵗʰ 1739-40 then was maried at Middleboʳ. Nathˡˡ. Washburne of Bridgwater & Mary Pratt of Middleboro. pʳ. me Benjᵃ White Just peace

Augᵗ. 11. 1740. Then was maried at Middleboro. Manaseh Donham of the Town of Plymouth & Sarah Hanks of Middleboro. pʳ. me Benjᵃ White Justice of peace

Augᵗ. the 26ᵗʰ. 1740. Then was maried at Middleboro. Willᵐ Lyon & Martha Knowlton both of Middleboro. pʳ. me Benjᵃ White Just peace

Septʳ. 1. 1740. Then was maried at Middleboro. Benjᵃ Washburn the 3ᵈ. & Zerviah Packard both of Bridgwater pʳ. me Benjᵃ White Just peace

Septʳ. 1. 1740. Then was maried at Middleboro. Willᵐ. Roach & Mary Kingman both of Bridgwater Pʳ me Benjᵃ White Just Peace

The Before written is Transcribed from Middleboro. Town Book by me Jacoᵇ Tomson Town Cler

[167] A list of middleborough marriages From 1740. To 1743-4—

June 2 1740 William Reed and Sarah Warren Both of middleborough were married at middleborough in The County of Plymʰ. pʳ. Benjᵃ. White Justice of peace

March 18. 1740-1 Samˡˡ. Pratt 3ᵈ. & Wibray Bumpas Both of middleboro. Were married at middleboro. in The County of Plymʰ.— — — pʳ Benjamin White Justice of peace

Novʳ. 5. 1741 Phineas Pratt and Sarah White Both of Middleborough Were married at middleborough in the County of Plymouth — — — pʳ. Benjamin White Justice of peace

Novʳ. 30. 1741 Ephraim Donham and mercy Tinkham Both of middleboro. Were married At middleboro. in the County of Plymʰ — — — pʳ. Benjᵃ. White Justice of peace

Decʳ. 31. 1741 Benjᵃ Warren and Jedidah Tupper Both of middleboro. in the County of Plymʰ. — — pʳ. Benjᵃ. White Justice of peace

January 28. 1741 Joseph Bumpas and mehitable Tupper Both of middleboro. Were married at middleboro. in the County of Plymʰ — pʳ. Benjᵃ. White Justice of peace.

[168] Aprill 1. 1742. Joseph Alden of middleborough and Hannah Hall of Bridgwʳ. Were married at middleboro. in yᵉ. County of Plymʰ — — — pʳ. Benjᵃ. White Jusᵗ. of peace

Aprill 1. 1742 Jacob Barden and Elinor Hackett Both of middleboro. Were married at middleboro. in the County of Plymʰ — — — Pʳ. Benjᵃ. White Just. of peace

may 24. 1742 Joshua Lazel and Elizabeth Ames Both of middleboro. Were married at middleboro. in yᶜ. County of Plymʰ. —— pʳ. Benjᵃ. White Justice of peace

octoʳ. 14. 1742 Samuel Thurber of Swanzey & Egatha Bryant of middleboro Were married at middleboro. in the County of Plymʰ — —— pʳ. Benjᵃ. White Justice of peace

octoʳ. 28. 1742 Israel Thomas and Phebe lyon Both of middleborough Were married at middleboro. in yᵉ. County of Plymʰ —— pʳ. Benjᵃ. White Justice of peace

Novembʳ. 11. 1742 Peter Walker of Taunton and Sarah Samson of middleboro. Were married at middleboro. in yᵉ. County of Plymʰ. —— pʳ. Benjᵃ. White Justice of peace.

Decembʳ. 20. 1742 Simon Lazel and Joanna Wood Both of middleboro. Were married at middleboro. in yᵉ. County of Plymʰ — pʳ. Benjᵃ. White Justice of peace

January 27. 1742-3 Jnᵒ. Tinkham Junʳ. and Jerusha Vaughan Both of middleboro. Were married at middleboro. in yᵉ. County of plymʰ —— pʳ. Benjᵃ. White Justice of peac

February 9. 1742-3 Jnᵒ. Harris and marcy Torrey Both of middleboro. Were married at middleboro. in yᵉ. County of Plymʰ. —— pʳ. Benjᵃ. White Justice of peac

Novʳ. 24. 1743 Jedediah Lyon and mary Cushman Both of middleboro. Were married At middleboro. in The County of Plymʰ —— pʳ. Benjᵃ. White Justice of peac

Decembʳ. 19. 1743 Jnᵒ. Thurber Junʳ. of Swanzey and Ann Bryant of middleboro. Were married at middleborough in yᵉ. County of plymʰ —— pʳ. Benjᵃ. White Justice of peace

February 16. 1743-4 Ichabod Wood and Thankfull Cobb Both of Middleboro. Were married at middleboro. — pʳ. Benjᵃ. White Justice of peace

February 21. 1743 Barnabas Eaton and Elizabeth Clemons Both of middleboro. Were married at middleboro. in yᵉ. County of Plymʰ —— pʳ. Benjᵃ. White Justice of peace

Aprill. 10. 1744 Jesse Bryant and Susanna Winslow Both of middleboro. Were married at middleboro. in yᵉ. County of Plymʰ —— pʳ. Benjᵃ. White Justice of peace

August. 10. 1743 Then I married Isaac Reynolds Junʳ. and mercy Niles Both of middleboro. —— pʳ. Benjᵃ. Ruggles ——

June 9. 1743 Then I married Josiah Richmond of Taunton and Elizabeth Smith of middleboro. —— pʳ. Benjᵃ. Ruggles ——

octoʳ. 6 1743 Then I married Joseph Richmond Junʳ. of Taunton and Elizabeth Hacket of middleboro. — pʳ. Benjᵃ. Ruggles

Novʳ. yᵉ. 4. 1743 Then I married mallachy Howland and Hopestill Dwelley Both of middleboro. ———— pʳ. Benjᵃ. Ruggles

February y^e. 16. 1743-4 Then I married Nathaniel Sprout and Esther Thrasher Both of middleborough —— —— p^r. Benj^a. Ruggles —— ——

The above & written written is a True Copy From middleborough Town Book   Seth Tinkham Town Clerk—

[169] 1738   A list of Bridgwater marriages From 1738. To 1742 —

July 13 David Whitman and Susanna Hayward —

oto^r. 11 Josiah Hayward and Sarah more —

Novr. 22 Eleazer Washburn and Anna Alden
     Ephaim Cary and Susanna Alden
     Ebenezer Byram and Abigal Alden
     Benajah Smith of Easton & Mary Hill of Bridgw^r.

Decr. 21 Seth mitchell and Ann Latham —
     26 James Radsford and margaret Bells – –

1739
march 27 Jonathan Allen of Braintry and y^e. widdow Alice Latham of Bridgwater

May 16 Samuel Harden and Elizabeth Wade

Novr. 20 Bridgwater and Cate Co^ll. Homans Negroes

Decr. 10 Charles Cushman and mary Harvey —
     21 Benjamin Vickory and mary kingman — were Joyned Together in wedlock p^r. The Rev^d. M^r. John Anger

1738
Jany. 4 John Pain and Hannah Pool —
     24 Caleb orcutt and mehetable Harvey

1739
aprill 19 Solomon Leach of Bridgwater and Jerusha Bryant of Plymton
     26 Jeremiah Conant and mary Packard —

may 10 John Freelove of Freetown and abigail Washburn Bridgwater
     23 Lieu^t. Daniel Hudson and The Widdow Abigail Fobes
     30 moses orcutt and mercy Allen —

Aug^st. 16 Thomas Drew of Hallifax and abigail Harris of Bridgwater

Novr. 27 Ebenezer leach of Bridgwater and Lydia Tillson of Plymton
     Joseph Whesley and Jean Gillmore

Jany. 1 Seth Alden and mehetable Carver
     3 Israel Washburn and Leah Fobes
     10 Benjamin Leach and Hannah keith
     24 Josiah Leonard and Jemimah Washburn

Feby. 6 Joseph Bolton and Deliverance Washburn
march 5 Josiah Fobes and Freelove Edson —
     6 Robert Washburn and Mary Fobes
    24 Nathaniel Bolton and The Widdow Deborah Ripley
1740
may 29 Joshua Fobes and Esther Porter
oct^r. 7 Elisha Hayward and Elizabeth Washburne
    22 Abraham Hardin of Bridgwater and Ruth Perry of
    Scituate
Novr. 7 Jonathan Benson and martha Snell were married p^r. The
    Rev^d. m^r. John Shaw
    11 Jonathan Pratt and Elizabeth French
Decr. 7 Henery Chamberlain and Susanna Hinds
Feby. 17 Israel keith and Betty Chandler
    19 Ephraim Holmes of Hallifax and margaret Washburn
    of Bridgwater
    24 Nehemiah Bryant of middleborough and Beth^h. Wash-
    burne of Bridgwater
[170]   1740
march 4 Robert keith and Tabitha Leach ——
    23 Jabez Cowing and Susanna Bolton were married By
    The Rev^d. m^r. John Shaw
1738
Septr. 26 Samuel Edson 3^d. and martha Perkins
Feby 27 Nathan Edson and mary Sprague – married p^r. Benj^a
    White Justice of peace
1741
May 13 John Cary and mary Harden married p^r. Dan^{ll}. John-
    son Justice of peace
1740
Septr. 16 Daniel Rickards and mary Packard and William Pack-
    ard and Sarah Rickards
1741
Aprill 28 Josiah Allen and Sarah orcut
May 20 Arthur Harris and Bethiah Hayward
June 23 Seth Whitman and Ruth Reed
Novr. 11 Jonathan Bass and Susanna Byram
Decr. 3 Ichabod Cary and Hannah Gannett
Jany. 6 Benjamin Hayward and Sarah Cary
    28 Daniel Cary and martha Cary were married By The
    Rev^d. m^r. Jno. Angier
1740
July 9 Jonathan mahurin and Widdow mary Packard
August 15 Ebenezer Kingman and Content Turner

1741
Aprill 2 Abisha Willis and Zeruiah Willis
Novr. 11 Thomas Willis and Susanna Ames were married By
     The Rev^d. m^r. Daniel Perkins
1741
Novr. 19 Benjamin Peterson of Easton and Hannah Perry of
     Bridwater married p^r. Daniel Johnson Justice of The
     peace——————
1742
Novr. 19 Joseph Peterson of Duxborough and Lydia Howell of
     Bridgwater married p^r. Dan^{el}. Johnson Justice of peace
June 4 Jessie Byram and abigail Thurston --
Augst 4 Hugh Orr and mary Bass
Novr. 9 Eleazer Whitman and Abigail Alden
     10 James Allen and Ann Pryer
     11 Zachariah Cary and Susanna Bass —
Decr. 13 Japhet Byram and Sarah Allen
     16 Joseph Alden and Susanna Packard
     John Whitman and Hannah Snow were married p^r. The
     Rev^d m^r, John Angier
A True Copy attest Jonah Edson Junr Town Clerk ————

[171] A List of Abington marriages From 1733. To 1742
Samuel Petingill and martha Jackson was married December y^e.
14. 1733
Jacob Reed and Hannah Noyes was married December The 21.
1733
Ebenezer Joslin and Easther Hersey was married June The 5.
1733
Samuel Pool and Rebekah Shaw was married November the 15.
1733
Jacob Ford and Sarah Pool was married November the 22. 1733
Hezekiah Ford and Deborah Beal was married November the
22. 1733
Eleazer Bate and Rachel Ager was married march 17. 1735
Nicholas Shaw and Ruth Beal was married February The 6.
1735
Peter Nash and mary Noyes was married November the 13. 1735
Jonathan Tory and Deborah Shaw was married December the
18. 1735
Joseph Pool and Ruth Ford was married November The 27.
1735
Benjamin Negro and Sarah Jonas was married march the 17.
1737

James Torey and Sarah Nash was married December The 25. 1735

John Reed and Abigail Niels was married December the 28. 1738

John Shaw and Lydia Shaw was married Aprill the 14. 1737

Samuel Reed and Elizabeth Hayward was married aprill the 28. 1737

James Richards and Hannah Shaw was married November. the 10. 1737

John Cobb and Ruth Chard was married February the 1. 1737

John Shaw and Silence Bate was married December The 14. 1738

Daniel Bate and Lydia Symmys December The 14. 1738

Peter Bate and Sarah Randall was married December the 14. 1738

William Tirrell and Hannah Whitmarsh was married January the 25. 1738-9

John Dyer and mary Reed was married aprill The 17. 1739

James Reed and Abigail Nash was married may The 10. 1739

Benjamin Edson and Anna Thayer was married october the 1. 1739

Samuel Noyse and Rebeckah Harden was married march the 3. 1736

Samuel Tirrell and Sarah Gurney was married November the 1. 1739

Barnabas Tomson and Hannah Porter was married march 13. 1740

James Rickards and Susana Pratt was married may the 15. 1740

Ephraim Spooner and Ruth Whitmarsh was married July The 24. 1740

James Reed and Ruth Pool was married august The 30. 1741

Alexander Nash and mary Tirrell was married october 22 1741

Isaac Tirrell and mary Whitmarsh was married october 22. 1741

Abraham Joslin and Rebeckah Tirrel married october 29. 1741

Jacob Reed and mary Ford was married November The 26. 1741

Edmond Jackson and Silence Allen was married February 24. 1741

Ezekiel Reed and Hannah Beal was married November 25. 1742

Andrew Ford and Sarah Shaw married November 25 1742

A True Copy of The Records of marriages in abington That Has Been Given in To me Ever Since I have Kept The Book of Records which Began in ye. year 1733

Transcribed By me
Jacob Reed Town Clerk

[172] A list of marshfield marriages From 1739 To 1743

Elnathan Fish of Kingston and Lydia Adams married Decemb^r. 12. 1739.

Thomas Ford and Jane Thomas of This Town were married Janu^y. 2 1739-40.

Michael Harny and Gail Rogers of This Town married January 14. 1739-40

Michael Samson of Kingston and Deborah Gardner of marshfield married February 1739-40

Seth Ewell and Jane Eames of This Town married February 21. 1739-40

Job Winslow and Elizabeth macumber were married march 20. 1740

Samuel Silvester and Sarah mori were married may y^e. 8. 1740

Benjamin Hatch Junr. of Scituate and mercy Phillips of This Town married June 25. 1740

Robert Shareman and The widdow mary Eames were married Septr. y^e. 23. 1740

Mathew Simonton of Falmouth and marcy oakman of this Town were married march 12. 1741

Benjamin Hatch of Scituate and Jerusha Phillips of This Town married aprill 7. 1741

Thomas Silvester and Hannah Harris married aprill 16. 1741 —

Elisha Kent and Susannah Ford married Jun y^e. 11. 1741

Elisha Rogers and margaret mackfarland married December y^e. 2. 1741

John Tilden the 3^d. and Rachel Hall married march y^e. 4. 1741

Derby Fits Patrick and Joanna Rogers married may y^e. 1. 1742

James Sprague Junr. and Patience Ford and Jno. Baker and Ruth Barker were married February The 24. 1742-3——

Benjamin White and Hannah Decro married aprill y^e. 3^d. 1743

Joseph Stetson of Scituate and mary Eames of this town married Septr. y^e. 15. 1743

James Lewis and Lydia Rogers of This Town married December y^e. 1. 1743

Ignatious Vinall of Scituate and mary Tilden of this Town married Decr. 15. 1743

A True list of The marriages Consummated Before me Atherton Wales.

5

Joseph Bruster of Duxborough and Jedidah White of marshfield were married Novr. 26. 1740

Ezekiel Kent and Susanna Winslow Both of marshfield were married Decem^r. 22 1740

John Tilden and Lydia Holmes Both of marshfield were married February 12. 1740

Nehemiah Thomas and Bial Winslow Both of this town were married July 6. 1741

Joseph Soul Junr. of Duxborough and mary Fullerton of marshfield were married march 18. 1742

Thomas Eames and margaret Dugles Both of marshfield were married June 10. 1742

William Winslow of middleboro. & Hannah Loe of marshfield were married Novr. 11. 1742

Snow Winslow and Lydia Crooker Both of marshfield were married Novr. 24. 1742

Jno. Tilden of Hanover and Sybil Thomas of marshfield were married Decr. 2. 1742

Robert Boath of Norwich and Lydia Hewett of marshfield were married march 21. 1743

Benj^a. Phillips and Else Thomas Both of marshfield were married Novr. 15. 1743

Jedediah Bourn and Sarah Thomas Both of marshfield were married octo^r. 24. 1743

Thomas Ford of marshfield and Hannah Turner of Pembrook were married Septr. 8. 1743

Amoss Ford and Lillis Turner Both of marshfield were married January 3. 1743-4

Thomas Little and Abigail Howland Both of This Town were married march 9. 1742

Jabez Whittemore and Elizabeth Howland Both of marshfield were married Sep^t. 26. 1743

p^r. me Samuel Hill Clerk

[173] A List of Kingston mariages from 1735. to 1734 viz. 1735

Octr. 2 — Joshua Sherman & Deborah Croade were maried

1736. Feby. 17. Joshua Bradford & Hannah Bradford were maried

1737. Jany. 11 Jon^a. Tilson and martha Washburn were maryed.

1742. Feby. 22 Cornelius White & Sarah Ford were maried.

april 26 Elisha Stetson jun^r. & Sarah Adams were maried.

1743. Sepr. 14 Thomas Phillips & Mary Mitchel were maried By me Nic^o Sever Just peace

1737. Decr. 15 Timothy morton & Mary Wilson were married.
1737. Feb. 23 Eben^r. Chandler & Anna his wife was maried.
1738. May 30. Charles Cooke & Hannah Faunce was maried.
1738 June 12. Andrew Samson & Sarah Phillips was maried
             Before me Joshua Cushing Just peace
1736 Jan^{ry}. 6 Peter Tinkham and Mary his wife was maried
             Before me Joshua Cushing J Peace
1736. June 26 James Claghorn & Elizabeth Ring was married.
1736. Octr. 21. John Simmons & Hopestil Stutson was maried.
    Octr. 21. Zachr^y. Chandler & Zerviah Holmes were maried
1736. Decr. 7. Nathan Wright & Hannah Cook was maried.
1736. Jany. 31 Edmund Hodges & mercy Cook were maried
1736 Augt. 18 John Wright & mercy Coomer was maried.
             Before Joseph Stacy
1737. Augt. 30. Samuel Wade & Mary Curtiss was maried.——
             Before Jo^s. Cushing Jus^t. peace
1742. Decr. 30. Abner Hall of Kingston to Sarah Hatch of
    Pembrooke
1742. Jan^{ry} 27 Benj^a. Eaton to Mary Tilson both of Kingston.
1743 apr. 5. J^{no}. Finney of Kingston to Betty Lovel of Abbing-
    ton
    May. 5. Eben^r. Morton to Susanna Holmes both of
    Kingston.
Novr. 25 Ichabod Bradford to Mary Johnson both of Kingston.
    David Eaton to Deborah Fuller both of Kingston
1744. June 27. Ignatius Cushing of Hallifax to Tabitha Fish
    of Kingston——————— were maried p^r. Thaddeus Mackarty
    Minister
    [191]—A List of Pembrooke mariages from 1738. To.
    1742. viz.
1 James Johnson of Scotland in Great Britain & Bethia Barker
    jun^r. of pembrooke were maried July 31. 1738.
2 Jonah Bisbee & Ruth Briant both of Pembrooke were maried
    Augt. 24th. 1738.
3 Willm. Richards of Pembrooke & Hannah Simmons of Dux-
    bor^o. were maried Sepr. 7. 1738
4 Richard Bordman of Duxbor^o. & Ester Samson of Pem-
    brooke negroes were maried Octr. 12. 1738.
5. Samuel Howland & Sarah Joy both of Pembrooke were
    maried Octr. 13. 1738.
6 William Curtis & Martha Macfarld Junr. both of Pembrooke
    were maried Novr. 14. 1738.
7 Henry Munroe of Swanzey & Hannah Joslyn jun^r. of Pem-
    brooke were maried Novr. 16 1738

8 Robert Stetson jun^r. of Scituate & Hannah Turner of Pembroke were maried Novr. 23. 1738.

9 Isaac Crooker & Desire Bates jun^r. both of Pemb : were maried Novr. 23. 1738.

10 Elisha Barker & Eliz^a. Bowen both of Pembrooke were maried Janr^y. 25 1738

11 Gideon Soule & Mercy Silvester both of Pembrooke were maried mar. 5th. 1738-9

12 Caleb Turner Junr. of Scituate & Ruth Briggs of Pembrooke maried May 1. 1739.

13 Francis Keen & Margret Hunt both of Pembrooke were maried Novr. 1. 1739

14. Richard Tillah a molatto & Peg a Negro Girl both Servants to M^r. Josiah Cushing of Pembrooke December 11th. 1739.

15. Solomon Russel & Dorothy Tubs were maried Decr. 27. 1739

16 Jno. Orcut of Bridgwater & Mary Webster of Pembrooke were maried mar. 31. 1740.

17 John Jordan of Scituate & Mercy Damon of Pemb. were mari^d. Decr. 23. 1740.

18. Nathaniel Baker & Susannah Lincoln jun^r both of Pemb. mar^d. Decr. 29 — 1740

19. Jno. Lincoln Junr. of Pemb. & Content Turner of Hanover maried Febr^y. 25. 1740.

20 Jno. Allen of Bridgw^r. & Bethia Crooker of Pemb. were maried Mar. 5. 1740

21 Hutson Bishop & Eliza Keen both of Pembrooke. maried Septr. 3. 1741

22 Nehemiah Cushing jun^r. & Sarah Humphreys both of Pemb. maried Novr. 18th. 1741.

23 Abr^a. Joslyn & Mary Soule both of Pemb. were maried Decr. 16. 1741.

24 Jno. Wallis of Pemb. & Eliz^a. Patteson of Hanover maried Decr. 29. 1741.

By the Rev^d. M^r. Daniel Lewis———

[192] 25 Joseph Ramsdell jun^r. of Pembrooke & mary Daws of Bridgwater were maried Decr. 30. 1741.—

26 Elisha Palmer of Hanover & Jerusha Stetson of Pembrooke were maried December 31. 1741.————

27 William Page & Agatha Stetson both of Pemb. were maried May 31. 1742

28 Joshua Brigs & Zervia Dellano both of Pemb: were maried June 3^d. 1742

29 Gideon Bisbee & Rebecca Turner both of Pemb. were maried Septr. 7. 1742.

30 Shubal Munroe & Mary Joslyn both of Pemb : were maried Novr. 10. 1742

31 Benj^a. Tailer of Hanover & Mery Russel of Pemb : were maried Decr. 23. 1742.
The above mariages were Consumated p^r. the Rev^d. M^r. Daniel Lewis————

32 Samuel Peirce & Rachel Cordwell both of Hanover were maried June 12. 1742.

33 Recompence Magoune & Ruth Crooker both of Pembrooke were maried July 20. 1742.

34 John Ransom of Kingston & Desire Bishop of Pembrooke were maried October 11th. 1742.

35 Job Simmons of Plimton & Abigail Parris of Pemb : were maried Octr. 20. 1742

36 Job Crooker & Abigail Winslow both of Marshfield Decr. 15. 1742

37 Nathl Croade & Eliz^a. Carter both of Plymouth were maried Decr. 29. 1742
By Joshua Cushing Justice of the peace A True Copy Transcribed from the Records of the Town of Pembrooke attest Daniel Lewis Junr. Town Cler

The following is a list of the marriages Solemnized by the reverend m^r. Jonathan Parker ——— viz.

1 Febr^y. 23. 1741. Robert Avery to Anna Cushman.

2 24 Isaac Lobdel to Ruth Clarke

3 and Thomas Loring unto Sarah Lobdel

4 May 12. 1742 Plilemon Samson unto Rachel Standish

5 June 9. 1742. David Darling unto Ruth Faunce

6 Novemb^r. 10. 1742. Asa Cook unto Susanna Bryant

7 11. 1742 Ichabod Churchel unto Rebecca Curtis

8 1. Benjamin Shaw unto Mary Attwood.

9 25. Ephraim Paddock unto Sarah Bradford

10 and Robert Cook unto Hannah Bisbe

11 april 7. 1743. Elkanah Cushman unto Hannah Standish

12 August 12. 1743. John Holmes unto Joanna Adams

13 October 6. 1743 Eleazer Richard unto Martha King.

14 Decr. 1. 1743. Simeon Holmes unto Abiah Stertevant

15 January 19. 1743. James Whiten Junr. unto Molly Lucas
Plymton February 20. 1743.
A True Copy p^r me Josiah Perkins Town Cler

A List of Mariages Solemnized by Edward Arnold Esqr Just peace viz.

1 July 20. 1738 Eliakim Willis of Dartmouth & Lydia Fish of Duxbor°.

2 December 12ᵗʰ 1738 Jethro Sprague & Patience Bartlett both of Duxbor°.

3 Decembr. 17. 1738 Miles Standish junr. of Duxbor°. & Mehitable Robins of Plym°.

4 March 1. 1738-9 Hezekiah Herrington & Hannah Southworth both Marshfield

5 Nathaniel Simmons & Mercy Simmons both of Duxbor° June 12ᵗʰ. 1739

6 Isaac Tinkham of Plym°. & Keziah Wormall Duxbor°. July 26. 1739

[193] 7 William Wilson of Scituate & Hannah Bourne of Marshfield Novr. 28. 1739

8 Decr. 3. 1739. Hezekiah Ripley & Abigail Hunt both of Duxborough

9 1739-40 March Eleazer Harlow of Duxbor°. & Abigail Thomas of Marshfield

10 May 22 1740. Nathˡˡ. Blackmer of Dartm°. & Rebecca Samson of Duxbor°. Maried

11 June 23. 1740. William Tolman of Scituate & Abigail Williamson of Marshfield

12 Novr. 4. 1741. Jedediah Soule & Tabitha Bishop both of Duxbor°.

13 July 8. 1742. Samuel Sprague junr. & Sarah Oldham both of Duxbor°.

14. Febry. 10. 1742-3 Benjᵃ Howland of Pembrooke & Experience Edgartown of Hallifax

15 Thomas Gullifer & Keturah Samson both of Duxbor°. Octr. 26. 1743.

16 Novr. 4. 1743. John Chandler 3ᵈ. & Sarah Weston Both Duxbor°.

The Following Mariages Solemnized by the Revᵈ. Mr. Samuel Veazie viz.

1. May 28. 1740 David Delano & Abigail Chandler both of Duxbor°.

2 May 31. 1740. Micah Soule & Mercy Southworth both of Duxborough

3 Decr. 31. 1740 Joseph Russel & Abigail Wadsworth both Duxbor°.

4 May 14. 1741 Abisha Sole & Abigail Delano both of Duxbor°.

5 July 9. 1741 Lemuel Delano & Lydia Bartlett both Duxbor°.

6 Octr. 8. 1741 Charles Rider of Plym°. & Rebecca Bartlett of Duxborough

7 Novr. 19. 1741 Briggs Allden & Mercy Wadsworth both of Duxbor°.

8 April 20. 1742 Simeon Curtis of Scituate & Asenath Sprague of Duxbor°.

9 June 10. 1742 Nathaniel Bartlett & Zenobe Wadsworth both of Duxbor°.

10 Janry. 14. 1742-3 Jonᵃ. Crooker junᵣ. of Pembrooke & Bethia Lowden Duxbor°.

11 March 17. 1743. Nero Negroman & Patience Indian Woman both Duxbor°.

The following Mariages were Consummated at Plymouth By Samuel Bartlett Just of yᵉ Peace ———— viz

1. Janry. 21 1735. James Wood & Deborah Fish both of Plymouth

2. June 13. 1738. Simeon Totman & Sarah Little John both of Plym°.

3. William Clarke & Experience Doty both of Plymouth

4. Augᵗ. 3. Edward Doten & Phebe Phinney both of Plymouth

Septr. 5. William Harlow & Hannah Bartlett both of Plymouth

6 March 21. 1738-9 Joshua Swift of Sandwich & Jane Faunce of Plymouth

7 David Morton & Rebecca Finney both of Plym°. May 8ᵗʰ.

8 John Jones & Sarah Barnes both of Plymouth Augᵗ. 18. 1740

9 April 16. 1741. Edward Sparrow & Jerusha Bradford both of Plym°.

10 June 30. Mʳ. Ezra Whitemarsh & Mʳˢ. Dorothy Gardner both Plym°.

11 July 3. Jonᵃ. Sanders of Warham & Elizᵃ. Tinkam of Plym°.

12 May 13. 1742. William Wood & Elizabeth Finney both of Plym°.

13 19. Ephraim Holmes & Sarah Finney both of Plymouth —

14 March 3. 1742-3 Peleg West & Lydia Keen both of Kingston

15 14. — Gideon Gifford of Rochester & Lois Jackson of Plymouth

16 July 7. Silvanus Bartlett & Martha Waite both of Plym°.

The above is a true Copy of Record from Plym°. Town book Attest Samˡˡ. Barlett Town Clerk

1743 June 7 Cornelius Holmes & Mary Doten both of Plym°. maried by Josiah Cotton Esqʳ Just peace

A true Copy of Record attest Samuel Bartlett Town Cler —

[194] Mariages Solemnized by the revrᵈ. Mʳ. Nathˡˡ. Leonard of Plym°. Viz.

1 June 14. 1742. Benj^a. Barnes & Experience Rider both of Plymouth
2 M^r. Samuel Veazie of Duxbor^o. & M^{rs}. Deborah Samson of Kingston Augt. 6. 1742.
3. Septr. 6. 1742. Barzilla Stetson & Ruth Kempton both of Plymouth
4 Robert Shattuck & Ruhama Cooke both of Plym^o. Septr. 9th. 1742.
5 The^o. Cotten & Martha Sanders both of Plym^o. Octr. 29. 1742.—
6 Lemuel Bartlett & Mary Dotey both of Plym^o. Novr. 25. 1742.
7 Henry Saunders Junr. of Warham & Mary Hambleton of Plym^o. Decr. 13. 1742.
8 Joseph Shurtleff & Sarah Cob both of Plym^o. Decr. 9th. 1742
9 Jan^{ry}. y^e. 13. 1742-3 Joseph Ruggles of Hardwick & Hanah Cushman of Plym^o.
10 Jan^{ry}. 20. 1742-3 Thomas Faunce 4th. & Sarah Bartlett both of Plym^o.
11 Job Hammond Negro, & Hannah Quoy Indian Febr^y. 17. 1742-3
12 March 10. 1742-3 Noah Bradford & Hannah Clarke both of Plym^o.
13 March y^e. 17. 1742-3 William Keen & Ruth Sergeant both of Plym^o.
14 May 2. 1743. Doct^r. Lazarus Lebaron & m^{rs}. Lydia Cushman both of Plym^o.
15 May 26. 1743. Jonah Whetemore of Charlestown & Mary Hatch of Plym^o.
16 May y^e. 30. 1743. Francis Perriss & Mary Thomas Indians —
17 Septr. 22. 1743. David Curtice of Scituate & Hannah Ward of Plymouth
18 Novr. 10. 1743. John Bradford of Plymton & Eliz^a. Holmes of Plym^o.
19 Decr. 8. 1743. M^r. Jno. Greenleaf of Boston & m^{rs}. Priscilla Brown of Plymouth
20 Peter Daniel & Sarah Waterman Indians Decr. 18. 1743. both of Plym^o.
21 Febr^y. 13. 1743-4 Amos Donham & Ann Mackleroy both of Plym^o.
22 Febr^y. 14. 1743-4 Ephraim Ward & Sarah Donham both of Plym^o.
23 Febr^y. 23. 1743-4 Gideon White of Marshfield & Joanna Howland Plym^o.
    A True Copy of Record from Plym^o. Town book——
    Attest Saml. Bartlett Town Cler

A List of Marriages by Edward Winslow of Rochester Just of peace viz.

1 April 10. 1740. Elisha Tupper & Mary Hommond both of Rochester.

2 Nov.r. 26. 1740. Daniel Wing & Mary Cliften both of Rochester.

3 Aug.t. 6. 1741. Marke Haskell y.e 3.d. & Elizabeth Witredge both of Plym.o.

4 Oct.o. 15. 1741. Jn.o. Penny of Harwick & Eliz.a. Dellano of Rochester.

5 Dec.r. 20. 1741. Simon Burge & Deborah Edwards both of Rochester

6 Samuel Rider Jun.r. & Mary Chapman both of Roch.r. April 13. 1742

7 Nov.r. 16. 1742. William Tereth & Dinah Dexter both of Rochester

8 March 15. 1742. Lemuel Claghorne & Deborah Wing both of Roch.r.

9 May 2. 1743. Elijah Caswell & Hannah Freman both of Rochester

10 July 12. 1743 Job King & Uniss Hammond both of Rochester

11 July 13. 1743 Joshua Lawrence & Jane Haskell both of Rochester

12 Oct.r. 20. 1743. Amos Mendal & Susanna Church both of Rochester.

13 January 4. 1743 Haneniah Gifford & Joanna Mendal both of Rochester

[195] 14 January 4.th. 1743 John Mattkelf & Rebecca Crapoo both of Rochester

15 Received Febry. 14. 1743. & Entered in Town Book of Records of Rochester
p.r Sam.ll. Wing T. Cler.

Peleg Dexter & Catherine Cosby both of Rochester were maried p.r Ivory Hovey Past.r.

[196] 1 Thomas Weeks of Hardwick & Katharine Clarke of Rochester were maried the 3.d. of April 1743.

2 George King & Lydia Snow were maried Aug.t. 4. 1743.

3 James Francis & Hosea Nummuch Ind.ns. Sept.r. 28. 1743.

6

4 David Paker of Newporte & Dorothy Robinson maried Oct⁰. 27. 1743.

5 Joseph Tharp & Charity Andrews maried Janrʸ. 1. 1743.

6 John Goodspeed & Mercy Hamond maried Febrʸ. 5. 1743.— by me Tim⁰. Ruggles.

Samuel Savory & Elizabeth Bumpas of Warham were maried December 25ᵗʰ, 1739. pʳ. me Timothy Ruggles.

A List of Marriages by mʳ. Rowland Thacher of Warham.

1 Septʳ. 6. 1741. Gersham Morss of Middlebor⁰. & Elizᵃ. Swift of Warham

2 Josiah Swift & Mary Besse both of Warham Novʳ. 19. 1741.

3 Decʳ. 9. 1741. Jonᵃ. Dillano of Rochʳ. & Rachel Bump of Warham

4 March 15. 1741-2 Josiah Man of Scituate & Mary Chubbuck of Warham

5 Daniel Raymond & Elizᵃ. Doty March 21. 1741.

6 Octʳ. 22. 1742. Hezekiah Bourne aged 65, & Mehitable Hinckley aged 25.——

7 Novʳ. 4. 1742. Joseph Landen Junʳ. & Sarah Lovell.

8 Novʳ. 3. 1743. Jonᵃ. Earle & Hannah Dotey.

9 Decʳ. 22. 1743. Joshua Besse & Lydia Sanders— were maryed pʳ. me Rowland Thacher

[199] Marshfield April 17. 1745. A List of Mariages Compleated before me Since December 15, 1743. viz.

1 Onesimus Macumber of this Town & Lucy Barker of Hingham were maried January 15. 1744.

2 Robert Cushman of Kingston and Prudence Sherman of this town were maried February 2ᵈ. 1744.

3 Elisha Sherman and Lydia Walker both of this town were maried Febrʸ. 5. 1744.

4 Jn⁰. Hamilton of Worster & Mercy Simenton of this town were Maried Febrʸ. 7. 1774 — - pʳ. Atherton Wales.—

[211] A List of Marshfield Mariages Solemnized by?

Thomas Phillips Junʳ, of Duxborough & Lydia Carver of this town were maried January 24. 1744-5.

Joseph Kent & Lydia Thomas were maried Febrʸ. 28ᵗʰ. 1743.

Jonathan King of Plimouth & Deborah Carver of this Town were maried Febrʸ. 21. 1744-5.

[212] A List of Mariages Solemnized by the Revᵈ. Mʳ. Samuel Veazie of Duxborough viz.—

1 John Sprague & yᵉ widdow Deborah Simmons Decʳ. 5. 1744.—

2 John Goold of Hull & Huldah Brewster of Duxbor⁰. June
   13. 1745.
3. Eleazer Harlow of Duxborough & Abigail Clarke of Plimouth
   were maried Sepʳ. 11. 1745.
4 Ichabod Simmons & Lydia Soule were maried Decʳ. 8ᵗʰ. 1743.
5 Thomas Prince of Kingston & Lydia Delano of Duxborough
   Decʳ. 8. 1743
   were maried p Samˡ Veazie
1 Jabez Cole & Grace Keen both of Duxbor⁰. were maried
   august 23ᵈ. 1744.
2 Amos Samson & Deborah Samson were maried Octʳ. 19.
   1744—
3. Ebenezer Delano & Lydia Wormall were maried May 16. 1745.
   Pʳ. Edward Arnold Just of peace

   [213] The following is a List of Mariages Consumated by
   Mʳ. Othniel Campbel

July 31. 1744. Ephraim Tilsen and Deborah Ransom both of
   Plimpton were maried —
September 25. 1744. Abraham Jackson of Plimouth & Bethiah
   Whitin of Plimpton were Joind together in Mariage——
January 4. 1744. Samuel Thomas of Middlebor⁰. & Mehitable
   Barows of Plimton were Joynd together in Mariage——
April 25. 1745 Mʳ. John Doten of Plimton & Hannah Sherman
   of Plimouth were Joynd together in mariage —
   Plimton Decʳ. 16. 1745. a true Copy pʳ. me Josiah Perkins
   Town Cler

   [226] A List of Mariages of the Town of Bridgwater—viz.
   1743
Novʳ. 30. Nathan Allen and Rebecca Reed.
Janrʸ. 18 Daniel Howell & Deliverance Latham
Febrʸ. 7 John Edson and Mary Gannet were Maried pʳ. the
   Revᵈ. Mʳ. John Angier
   1743
April 13. Isaac Lathroop and Patience Alger.
May 5 Thomas Wade & Elizᵃ. Hanmer
   26. David Johnson & Susannah Willis
   1744.
April 19 Daniel Lathroop and Rhoda Willis
   were Maried pʳ. Danˡ. Johnson Esqʳ
   1741.
April 21 Elijah Edson and Ann Packard.
May 4 James Clansey and Ruth Ballancy.

26 Eben[r]. Leach of Bridgwater & Mary Wilbore of Raynham
    — Benanuel Leach & Betty Perkins —
July 29. Ruben Hall & Ruth Gilbert
Aug[t]. 11 Stoughton Willis and Hannah Harlow
Oct[r]. 12 William Leach & Mary Cohoone
Dec[r]. 3. M[r]. Eliab Byram & M[rs]. Phebe Leonard
    22 Joseph Wilbore of Raynham & Susanna Harris of Bridg-
    water.
    — Benj[a]. Pratt & Lydia Harlow
Febr[y]. 11 Josiah Hayward & Mary Perkins
Mar. 5. James Wickett & Betty Moses Indians
1742.
May 5. James Perkins & Bethiah Dunham
June 3 Jonathan Allen of Brantrey & Mary Latham Bridgwater
    [227] July 20. Ezra Washburne and Susanna Leach —
Aug[t]. 5. William Gilmore and Margarett Stewart
Oct[r]. 25 Samuel Bolton Bridgwater and Rebecca Simmons
    Hallifax
1743.
April 5. Nathaniel Hayward Bridgwater & Eliz[a]. Curtiss Hallifax
Sep[r]. 29 Jabez Carver & Sarah Perkins
    — Abraham Perkins & Mary Carver
Oct[r]. 17 Benjamin Price & Silence Hayward
Nov[r]. 3 Benjamin Peirce of Scituate & Charity Hayward of
    Bridgwater
    — 7 William Snow & Hannah Hill
Dec[r]. 20 Isaac Pool & Sarah Leonard
Jan[ry]. 12 Arthur Bennet of Middlebor[o]. & Keziah Keith of
    Bridgwater
    — 24 Jonathan Allden & Experience Hayward
Febr[y]. 17. Lot Conant of Bridgwater & Betty Homes of Middle-
    bor[o].—
March. 8 Robert Hoar of Middlebor[o]. & Sarah Willis of Bridgw[r].
1744
April 10. Joseph Hayward of Raynham & Mary Cahoone of
    Bridgwater
June 14 Daniel Keith & Elizabeth Conant
Sep[r]. 20. Joseph Bozworth of Hallifax & Sarah Cobb of Brigw[r].
Nov[r]. 15 Abiezer Edson & Mary Packard.
    — 24 Joseph Cowing of Scituate & Jean Keith of Bridgw[r].
Dec[r]. 10. Nathan Kingsley of Easton & Betty Dunbar of Bridgw[r].
Mar. 4. Joab Willis and Martha Bolton

Were maried by the rev^d. m^r. John Shaw
1741.
Mar. 1 Joel Edy & Rachel Vosse
1742. Novr. 11 Jacob Hayward & Tabitha Hayward
1743.
April 21. James Stacey of Easton & Mehitable Willis of Brigw^r.
July 19 Thomas Willis of Taunton & Bethiah Hayward of Bridgw^r.
Augt. 26. William Hall & Ann Chasta
Octr. 13. Benoni Hayward & Hannah Page
1744
June 14 Seth Thayer & Hannah Pray.
Novr. 22. Oliver Cheney of Pomphret & Hannah Hayward of Bridgw^r.
Decr. 3. James Linsey & Hannah Turner
were maried by the Rev^d. M^r. Danl. Perkins.
1744
May 28. Robert Dawes & Lydia Harden
June 7. Joseph Gannet and Betty Latham
Sepr. 27. Naphtali Byram and Hannah Pratt
were maried by the Rev^d. M^r. John Angier
A True Copy from the Town Record Examined
p^r Josiah Edson jun^r. Town Cler

[228] The following Couples were Maried in Middleborough by me the Subscriber at the times perticulerly Mentioned (Viz)
Nathan Bennet and Jemima Samson both of Middlebor^o. Decr. 5.
1745.
Eben^r. Briggs of Taunton & Margerey Leonard of Middleb^o. February 6. 1745-6
Thomas Weld Minister of the Gospel in Middleborough

Decr. 13. 1745 Then John Hall & Lydia Hacket both of Middlebor^o. was maried
Jany. 2. Then m^r. Saml. Southworth & m^rs. Eliz^a. Caswell Junr. were maried
     By me Benjamin Ruggles.
     The above written is a True Copy Transcribed from Middlebor^o. Town Book —— Attest Jacob Tomson Town Cler.
     [230] Marshfield July 7th. 1746. A List of Persons maried by me Samuel Hill Clerk.——
Benjamin Barnes & Mary Gullifer were maried Sepr. 16. 1745.
M^r. Anthony Thomas of this Town & M^rs. Abigail Allden of Duxborough were maried Jan^ry. 23. 1745-6——

John Fullerton of this town & Rebecca Dellano of Duxbor⁰. were maried April 17ᵗʰ. 1746

Anthony Sherman & Silence Foord were maried April 17ᵗʰ. 1746.

[231] Marriage Consummated by the Revᵈ. Mʳ. Jonathan Ellis —

1740.

Augᵗ. 24. Ebenezer Harlow & Meriah Morey both of Plimouth marryed a Ditt⁰.

Novʳ. 13. Nathaniel Morton & Mary Elles both of Plimouth married at D⁰.

Febrʸ. 19 Jonᵃ. Tobey of Sandwich & Deborah Swift of Plimouth marryed at Plim⁰.

1742. Mar. 18. Thomas Clarke & Ruth Morton both of Plimouth marryed at D⁰.

April 22. Jonathan Harlow & Sarah Holmes both of Plim⁰. marryed at D⁰.

1743. Augᵗ. 11. Joseph Morton the third & Experience Morton both of Plim⁰. marryed.

Sepʳ. 29 Edward Tinkham of Kingston & Lydia Rider of Plim⁰. married at Plim⁰.

Decʳ. 14. Eleazer Holmes Junʳ. & Esther Ellis both of Plim⁰. married a D⁰.

1744. Mar. 11 Joseph Croswell of Groton & Jerusha Bartlett of Plim⁰. married at D⁰.

Novʳ. 29. Joslyn Sepit & Joanna Sepit Indians both of Plim⁰. married a D⁰.

1745. Apr. 11 Ebenʳ. Holmes the 3ᵈ. & Susanna Holmes both of Plim⁰. marryed at D⁰.

1744. Augᵗ. 5 William Fish & Mercy Morey both of Plimᵉ. maryed a D⁰.

Mariage Solemnized by Samuel Bartlett Esqʳ Just Peace for the County of Plimouth.

1744-5. Joseph Fulgham & Rebeccah Young both of Plym⁰. March 1

1745.

Sepʳ. 26. Jacob Decoster & Elizᵃ. Cole both of Plimouth marryed at D⁰.

Mariages Consummated by the Revᵈ. Mʳ. Nathaniel Leonard.

1745.

April 11 Elkanah Shaw of Middlebor⁰. & Joannah King of Plim⁰. marryed.

—25 Eleazer Donham of Plimpton & Phebe Lucas of Plim⁰. married a D⁰.

July 28. Jire Fish of Sandwich & and Hannah Finney of Plim°. married

Augt. 15 Caleb Sherman & Rebecca Rider both of Plim°. marryed at D°.

Sepr. 10. Azariah Whiten of Plimton & Rebecca Holmes of Plimouth marryed a D°.

1745-6. 23. Joseph Churchel & Meriah Rider both of Plim°. maryed a D°.

Febr^y. 10. Stephen Doten & Hannah Bartlet both of Plim°. maried at D°.

Mar. 6. Benj^a. Delano of Duxbor°. & Lydia Jackson of Plim°. marryed a D°.

Mariages Solemnized By the Rev^d. M^r. Thomas Frink of Plim°.

1745.

Octr. 3. Daniel Robins & Sarah Sanders Indians of Plim°. marry'd at D°.

Octr. 4. Thomas Ling & Eliz^a. Mackfun both of Plim°. marryed a D°.

— 31 Amaziah Churchel & Eliz^a. Silvester both of Plim°. marryed a D°.

1745-6. Febr^y. 25. Thomas Burge & Patience Dotey both of Plim°. maried a D°.

1745-6 A True Copy of Record attest Samuel Bartlet Town Clerk

Peleg Sprague &   Chanler both of Duxborough were Joyned together in Marriage

Samuel Winsor & Rhoda Delano both of Duxborough were Joyned together in mariage

     By me Edward Arnold Just Peace

[232] Mariages Consummated by Elijah Cushing Esqr one of the Justices of the Peace for the County of Plimouth viz.

1736.

Augt. 23. William Estes of Hanover & Eliz^a. Stetson of Scituate were maried

Sepr. 30 Andrew Linsey & Ruth Parrish both of Pembrooke were maried

1737. June 1. John Barker of Hanover & Grace Turner of Scituate were maried

1738 June 29. Ebenezer Rogers & Sarah Stetson both of Marshfield were maried

1739 July 4 Ebenezer Woodward & Hannah Stetson both of Hanover were maried

1740. July 8. Shedrak Keen & Eliza. Turner both of Hanover were maried

1741 July 2. Caleb Rogers of Scituate & and Mary Harlow of Hanover were maried

1742 June 30 James Hanks of Pembrooke & Abigail Phillips of Bridgwr. were maried

Janry. 27. Theophilus Cushing & Hannah White both of Pembrooke were maried

1743. Janry. 11 Silas Stetson & Mary Brackit both of Scituate were maried

1744 Janry. 29. Joshua Staples of Hanover & Eliza. Conaway of Pembrooke were maried

March 7 Ebenezer Record & Joanna Bowls both of Pembrooke were maried

1746. Sepr. 19. Prince Palmer of Scituate & Ruth Bowker of Hanover were maried
pr. Elijah Cushing Just Peace

The following Mariages were Consumated by the Revd. mr. Benja. Bass of Hanover — viz.

1744
March 29. Joshua Ripley & Alice Stetson both of Hanover were maried

April 28 Eleazer Donham of Plimouth & Eliza. Conner of Hanover were maried.

Decr. 6. Jesse Torrey & Mary Buker both of Hanover were maried

1746. May 31 Daniel Cotherel of Bridgwr. & Hannah Rose of Hanover were maried
pr. me Benja. Bass Pastr. of Hanover

[236] 1 Nathan Pratt & Sarah Harlow were maried Octr. 15. 1745——

2 Benja. Benson & Keziah Snell Octr. 30. 1745——

3 Thomas Thomson & Jane Washburne Octr. 31. 1745 —

4 Thomas Conant & Mary Wood Octr. 29. 1745.

5 Nathl. Pratt & Hannah Conant Novr. 5. 1745

6 Eleazer Cary & Betty Fobes Novr. 12. 1745.

7 Elijah Leach & Jemima Snow Decr. 4. 1745.——

8 James Dunbar & Hannah Benson Janry. 22. 1745 —

9 Josiah Washburne & Abigail Curtiss Janry. 29. 1745 —
[237] 10 Eleazer Carver junr. & Hepsiba Perkins April 3. 1746—

11 John Sprague & Susanna Cob June 20 : 1746 —

www.ingramcontent.com/pod-product-compliance
Lightning Source LLC
Chambersburg PA
CBHW051711090426
42736CB00013B/2649